MY HUSBAND DOESN'T LOVE ME

And He's Texting Someone Else

MY HUSBAND DOESN'T LOVE ME

And He's Texting Someone Else

The Love Coach Guide to Winning Him Back

ANDREW G. MARSHALL

MARSHALL METHOD
PUBLISHING

MARSHALL METHOD
PUBLISHING

A Marshall Method Publishing Paperback

Marshall Method Publishing
London • Florida
www.marshallmethodpublishing.com

ISBN 978-0-9574297-3-4

Library of Congress Cataloging-in-Publication Date is available
through the Library of Congress.

Cover design: Gary A. Rosenberg • www.thebookcouple.com
Interior design: Elspeth McPherson • www.whitebeamdesigns.co.uk

Printed in the United States of America

10   9   8   7   6   5   4   3   2   1

To Elena,

who has been looking forward to this book

"My husband used to tease me about reading all your books and taking a psychology masters course. During such a discussion, I threw at him that I was just preparing to write a book myself: My Husband Doesn't Love Me Anymore and He's Texting All the Time. Of course, he is quite intrigued at the coincidence of your new book. I can't wait to offer it to him as a present. I am sure it will be a bestseller; texting around and messing up potentially good relationships has turned into quite a phenomenon."

CONTENTS

It is ten years since the first person arrived in my marital therapy room having told their partner: "I love you, but I'm not in love with you." I wrote an article for the *Observer* newspaper in the UK about couples splitting up, not because they hated each other but because one partner had fallen out of love.

The response was overwhelming and I was asked to write the book: *I Love You But I'm Not in Love with You: Seven steps to saving your relationship.* It turned out to be not just a UK phenomenon: the book has been translated into German, French, Italian, Chinese, Japanese, Swedish, Greek, Turkish—in fact, fifteen languages and counting. I was also the first UK-based self-help writer to be published by HCI Books in the USA (the publishing house behind the bestselling "Chicken Soup for the Soul" series).

Back in 2006, when the book was published, I thought I'd written everything that needed be said on "I love you, but ...." However, it was aimed at both the person who had fallen out of love and their partner. I didn't cover the differences between when a woman falls out of love and when a man falls out of love, because I didn't want to make generalizations about all women this or all men that. My sample of cases were all couples who were committed enough to saving their relationship to phone up Relate (the UK's leading couple-counseling charity), book an appointment for an initial assessment, and wait the weeks and sometimes months to start on-going counseling. However, desperate letters to my website (www.andrewgmarshall.com) told a different story—about men and women who had told their partners they'd fallen out of love and either immediately or a few days later declared that the relationship was over. They couldn't "change" their feelings, they needed "space," and the children "should be told." There was "no point" going into counseling and if the person who had fallen out of love did reluctantly

1

agree, it was only to tick a box that "we tried everything." These correspondents had found my book incredibly helpful and drawn hope from my message that "you can fall back in love again," but wanted to know how to communicate this to their partner.

The more letters I received and the more stories I heard, I began to realize that it was a completely different experience being a man, rather than a woman, being told "I love you, but …." Time and again, these men were isolated and didn't know where to turn for support. They had always taken their emotional problems to their wives. They had friends, but they were more likely to offer a beer than advice or a chance to talk. So I decided to write a book aimed specifically at men, *My Wife Doesn't Love Me Any More*, to help with their sense of isolation, to offer emotional support and to provide a practical program for rescuing their relationships.

I thought women didn't need a book specifically targeted at them. They have plenty of friends to offer support and, while media aimed at men is full of sport, politics, and business, women's magazines, TV programs and websites are overflowing with relationship advice. However, sometimes, these pluses turn into negatives. Talking to friends can fan the flames of panic and lots of women have told me that they don't want to confide in their friends (who sometimes turn them into a living soap opera). Although it's great to have lots of heartfelt advice—from magazines and the internet—it's often contradictory or falls into the "dump him" or "all men are cheaters" category. Obviously, that's not much help if you still love your husband and desperately want to save your marriage.

I knew I had to write a book targeted specifically at women, when I counseled one couple where the wife was so consumed by anger that she could not hear the underlying messages from her husband. Certainly, on the surface, they sounded bleak: "I don't know what I want" and "I'm not certain that we can rescue our marriage." He had also moved out of the house because he couldn't stand the rows anymore. In their counseling sessions, the angrier she became the more he disappeared into his shell. The less he said, the more her overactive imagination stepped into the breach. Instead of asking what he felt, she told him what he felt (and found the most negative interpretation possible). Not surprisingly, her husband either became defensive or thought "what's the point" and in the counseling sessions he clammed up, and during the rest of the week hung up the phone on her or walked away.

However, when she was calmer, she began to interpret everything in a slightly more nuanced way. When he said 'I don't know what I want," she could reply "I'm not certain either because all this is doing my head in too" and we were able to build a small bridge toward recognizing their similarities and starting to work as a team. At this point, she could also look past "I'm not certain that we can rescue our marriage" to something more positive: "we are still talking and actively trying to turn this relationship around." However, all too often her righteous anger (because she had been hurt and rejected) would often tip over into ranting (which simply made her husband clam up again) and her helpful desire to understand would tip into overanalyzing (which made her either panic or despair). All too often, a breakthrough in resolving a tricky issue—for example weekend access to the children—would be undone during the week by her fears and anxieties. At this point, I realized that she needed not just weekly counseling but coaching too.

So what's the difference? Counseling is about helping someone open up, explore their feelings, and ultimately to find their own solutions. It works best when the peak of a crisis is over and the dust has settled a bit. However, my female client did not need to "get in touch" with her anxiety, but to manage it better. And that's where coaching comes in. Coaching is about sharing knowledge (gained from previous experience in the trenches of a problem). It offers practical suggestions and helps you to rehearse your messages to your partner. Ultimately, coaching is about keeping you calm, focused, and stopping you from turning a crisis into a disaster.

In an ideal world, if your partner has fallen out of love, you should be in couple counseling together, working through the issues, as well as getting individual emotional support. Unfortunately, we don't live in an ideal world. However, my book *I Love You But I'm Not in Love with You* could be your couple counseling and this book your personal love coach. (When I counsel women face-to-face, I often write down key ideas to take away from the session and I've done something similar with the "Love Coach's Three Key Things to Remember" at the end of each chapter.)

Ultimately, it doesn't matter if you read Part One of this book or *I Love You But I'm Not in Love with You* first. However, if you're holding both in your hands (or have them on your e-reader), I would read *I Love You But I'm Not in Love with You* first. It provides a good introduction to many of the techniques that I will be using in this book but, more importantly, I would like you to read it before handing it over to your husband. (If he's not a reader, I have recorded an audiobook version.) In this way, if he is willing to read or listen to it, you'll be able to discuss any points that he raises and do the exercises together.

Moving onto Part Two of the book where I look at whether there's another woman on the scene and how to combat her influence, it's six years since I wrote *How Can I Ever Trust You Again?* to spread the word that marriages can recover from infidelity and couples can build stronger and better relationships. To be honest, I thought I'd covered almost everything that needed to be said about infidelity too. However, I still worked for Relate and we tended to see people after the immediate crisis had passed. In other words, the affair had been discovered but the couple were committed enough to their relationship to book an appointment and go on a waiting list, before finally starting work with me. I hardly ever saw people right in the eye of the storm: unsure whether their partner would stay or go or whose partner kept denying there'd even been any wrongdoing. However, desperate letters to my website told of the drama of packed and then unpacked bags, the gut-wrenching pain of being home alone while your partner was out womanizing, and the frustration of knowing that something distasteful was happening while your partner was flatly denying it.

Many of my correspondents were having counseling—and it helped take the edge off their pain—but they needed something more. They each wanted to understand what was going on inside their partner's head; they needed advice on how to communicate more effectively and how to keep calm while the world was conspiring to turn them mad. In other words, they needed coaching as much as counseling.

There's another reason why I've decided to write this book. My casebook for *How Can I Ever Trust You Again?* was based mainly on infidelity in the late 1980s and early 1990s. For much of that time, it was easier to draw the line under an affair. Cell phones were rare and the internet was something for geeks. However, in the years since I wrote the book, smartphones have become standard and social networking has taken off and added a whole new complexity, with the affair partner (or ex-affair partner) able to come into your home at any time—via text, email, tweet, or Facebook message. With 24/7 communication, if your partner's resolution slips for just a moment, he can be in contact instantly with the other woman and your marriage drops down into a fresh circle of hell. So while in the past, the journey to recovery might have been stop-and-start, today it can seem like you're constantly being sent back to the beginning (or never even leaving it).

Although I don't have any easy answers, I can break your problems down into more manageable chunks. I can help you to keep hold of your sanity, can explain your options and advise on when to make a strategic withdrawal and when to fight on.

If the affair has supposedly ended, I would read *How Can I Ever Trust You Again?* first—even though you suspect or fear that your husband and the other woman are still in contact. It will give you a better idea of the journey ahead and of whether the pitfalls are part of the natural recovery process or because the affair has been rekindled.

If your partner will not admit to an affair, has confessed (or made a partial confession) but doesn't know what he wants, or is determined to leave with his new "love," please start with this book because it focuses on finding a way through an immediate crisis.

How to use this book

Although this book is called *My Husband Doesn't Love Me and He's Texting Someone Else* it will help even if there is not another woman involved. It's perfectly possible that your husband feels that his life has hit a brick wall, he's tried to sort out his unhappiness and you've either failed to hear how serious he is (and despite trying harder everything's slipped back to normal) or he's kept his problems to himself. Perhaps he's depressed and feels leaving and starting again is the only viable option.

However, over the past thirty years, I've counseled thousands of men and women who have fallen out of love and, while only a minority of women are involved with another man, the majority of men are "getting advice" or "involved" to some degree with another woman. Some husbands will have stepped over the boundary from imagining what life might be like with her into sending flirty texts, developing an emotional attachment, or even starting a full-blown affair.

Whatever the circumstances, it still feels incredibly bleak: he doesn't see a future together, he wants to tell the children, and to split up your happy family.

Fortunately, I have a message of hope. It is possible to turn around your relationship and build a better and stronger marriage. However, it is important that you stay calm, listen to what he's saying, and not let overthinking turn a problem into a full-blown crisis. So even if there is another woman on the scene, please don't skip Part One, because it will explain how you got to this point—and the building blocks for rescuing your relationship are the same whether there is someone else or not. If you just suspect another woman, please give your husband the benefit of the doubt while you're reading Part One, since it will make it easier to step into his shoes and understand him. It will also help you to take this situation not quite so personally. OK, I know that's a tough ask. Of course, it feels personal: *he doesn't love you.* But this crisis says just as much about him: how he deals with problems and conflict, and how he was brought up. I know it's hard to feel compassionate toward your husband—especially as you long just to shake some sense into him—but it will pay dividends. If you can be kinder to your husband, you are also going to be kinder on yourself too and that's important because the journey is going to be tough.

If your husband has spoken up before his unhappiness tipped

over into some form of betrayal or you've spotted the problems early enough to nip it in the bud, there is no need to torture yourself by reading Part Two. If you are unlucky enough to find your husband has become emotionally attached to another woman, Part Two of this book will prove invaluable. If it's another *man*, I've written a special appendix, which includes other women's experiences and my advice.

An apology

I have used the word "husband" rather than "partner" in the title because I wanted to immediately indicate that this book was targeted at women. However, let me be clear: this book is for all women in committed relationships—whether married or not.

I have also had to make some blanket statements about men and women—even though I know there are countless exceptions. Having said that, there is often truth in generalizations. So even if something strikes you as "yes but ...," please be patient with me because even if you don't fit precisely into this category, it will illuminate how you might be coming across to your partner, and sometimes an extreme example will demonstrate more clearly what may need to be changed.

Andrew G. Marshall

www.andrewgmarshall.com

PART ONE

My Husband Doesn't Love Me

CHAPTER ONE

Help! My husband has fallen out of love

"We have been together since we were 17, we are now 38 and have been married for 12 years, with two beautiful children, ten and six. I always thought we had such a good marriage, not perfect by any means, but felt that we were giving it a good go. When my husband told me he didn't love me, it came as such a shock— not only to me, but everyone who knows us. The reasons he gave were incredible, he said I had changed since my mom died suddenly. He criticized me for wanting to keep the house tidy. I am a full-time mom, so felt that was my job. I suggested coming to counseling with me, but he refused and arranged to stay with his parents.

The night before he told the kids, I asked if he wanted to give it an another go, but he simply said no. I am heartbroken and devastated, as are the children. I still love him and want more than anything for us to save this marriage."

Your husband has turned into a stranger. The man you thought you knew has told you "I don't love you anymore" or maybe he's not actually said those words, but everything about his behavior screams it. He's moody, detached, and you feel like you're walking on eggshells all the time. How could this be? But we were supposed to be together forever? He doesn't love me? What have I done to deserve this?

Even if you knew the two of you had problems or if your marriage has come under a lot of pressure lately, you never imagined it would come to this. OK, perhaps in the back of your mind you knew that things weren't perfect or that you needed to "work" on your relationship, but you'd thought the upcoming vacation, your youngest child going off to school, or his retirement would mean you'd have more time together and sort something out. Except he's not interested in fixing your relationship; he either

11

shrugs his shoulders and disappears or he gets angry and tells you "if you don't know what the problem is, there's simply no point in talking."

Maybe he has told you what's the matter but his reasons don't make any sense—for example why would someone throw away years of marriage because you're always arguing with your daughter or, for example, how could he accuse you of "being controlling" when all you've ever wanted is the best for your family. Even if he does have a list of justified complaints that could be sorted—for example, he doesn't get enough time to go fishing, your sex life is in a rut, or you never go out together anymore—he simply says it's "too late" or he's "confused" and "doesn't know what he really wants," or perhaps he's just shut down and tells you to "stop going on about it."

Meanwhile, you're trying to be nice: you're offering to wear that lingerie he bought you for Christmas, you're ready to talk whenever he suggests, or backing off and giving him space. However, whatever strategy you try it has the same result: you're banging your head against a brick wall. His feelings have changed. It's too late. He doesn't love you anymore. Except that in the next minute, he's just "confused" or doesn't know what he wants. You can see he's hurting, but you don't know how to reach him. No wonder: you're exhausted, confused, and alternating between wanting to scream at him or to ask him to hold you and say "we'll get through this."

With any luck, you've got good friends who will listen and sympathize. Unfortunately, many friends will weigh in with advice: "there's another woman"; "he's having a midlife crisis"; "men are bastards." They tell you: "don't take it lying down"; "how could he do this to you"; "you need answers." OK, you'll feel better for a while because you'll have a label for this problem, a new sense of purpose, or you'll simply feel understood. Except the reassurance and the positive mood is soon scuppered by some unreasonable behavior by your husband; trying to get him to open up just makes him retreat deeper into his shell and get angry; and accusing him of a midlife crisis or an affair pushes your marriage farther into crisis.

My guess is that you're full of despair, fear, and hopelessness.

Why else would you reach for a self-help book? I don't know your husband. I can't fully understand the ins and outs of your marriage. However, I have spent almost thirty years working with couples in crisis, helping women understand men better, and explaining women to men. So I can make a pretty good guess what's gone wrong in your marriage and I've some straightforward strategies for fixing, not only the surface stuff, but the long-term problems that eat away at the foundations of happy relationships. Even if there is somebody else on the scene, I will help you to assess how serious the situation is and the best approach for dealing with her. Ultimately, my goal is to help you to make judgments with both your heart and your head. How does that sound? Hopefully, good, so let's get started.

Is there any hope?

If I had a dollar for every time I've been asked this question, I'd be a rich man. So let's face the issue straight on:

> *"My husband thinks it's too late and there's been too much pain for our marriage to survive. He says he has a fond regard for me, but has probably been putting barriers up for two years and withdrawing from our relationship. He escapes with his mates on his motorbike when I try to hold our marriage together. He doesn't view the future with me in it. I think we may be classic 'I love you, but I'm not in love with you.' The more I've tried, the more he says he's realized he doesn't love me and he doesn't think we can get it back. Is there any hope? Is it savable? I can't bear to tell our kids."*

I know the situation seems bleak and this is certainly not going to be a quick fix. However, as you will find out, that's an advantage, not a disadvantage. If you're like most couples, it will be quick fixes that have got you into this mess in the first place and made the current crisis a whole lot worse. It is possible to turn things around and win back your husband—as long as you are prepared to look past the surface problems and meet at least two of the following criteria:

- *You and your husband, or partner, have been together for three years or more.* You need enough time to have come out of the honeymoon phase and for your relationship to have put down some solid roots. Of course, it helps to be married—because this shows a public commitment to being a couple—but some other demonstration of lasting affection, for example buying a home together, is enough.

- *You have children together.* Nobody with children will split up lightly. However, more importantly, day-to-day discussions about your son and daughter's needs or, if you are separated, picking them up and dropping them off provides plenty of contact time and the opportunity to try out the suggestions in this book. Some people worry that they might be staying together only for the children—I have to stress that's not what I'm suggesting—but learning to communicate better as parents can translate into communicating better as partners. Other people worry that they might be "using" their children, but as most parents' relationship reaches an "I love you, but ..." stage because of the stress of bringing up kids, it seems only fair that they can provide an opportunity to save it too.

- *You truly love him and want to win him back.* If it is just your pride that has been dented or you're worried about how you'll make ends meet or the impact on the kids, you will not have either the generosity needed for my program or the determination to keep going through the setbacks. Although your relationship can be saved, the journey ahead is not going to be easy. It involves learning a lot about yourself (some of it might be hard to accept) and making lasting changes (rather than a quick fix and hoping for the best).

- *You don't panic.* This is perhaps the toughest criteria. Of course you're going to panic. Your husband doesn't love you anymore; you're going to be able to afford only food marked down because it's reached the expiration date; and the children will be scarred for life! However, the more you panic, the more you will do stupid things that push him farther away. Equally importantly, the more you panic, the angrier you'll get and that's the point at which you'll tip over from righteous indignation—because he's said something hurtful or been selfish—into ranting at him—which makes men switch off or walk out the door. Don't worry, I've got lots of techniques to help you to stay calm, rational, and focused, but it will also take commitment and determination from you. In my experience, more relationships break down at this point because of the wife's panic, rather than the husband's determination to leave. Please remember this when you're feeling low.

Six worst reactions to discovering your husband doesn't love you

Hearing your husband say that he doesn't love you is horrible. You're bound to be upset. You will have probably said and done things that you now regret. In the long run, it doesn't matter how you reacted to his initial declaration. What really counts is how you've behaved in the subsequent discussions—during the hours, days and weeks afterward. In many cases, men progress from "I love you, but I'm not in love with you," to "I don't love you anymore" and then "it's over," because women fall into one or more of the following traps.

Yes, but ...

It seems so incredible that your husband doesn't love you and so difficult to get your head around the idea that you've dismissed or downgraded the whole idea. Yes, you accept that "mistakes have been made" and there are lots of things that you regret, but in your rush to defend yourself, explain the background, or present a more balanced picture, you've responded with "Yes, but ...." For example: "*Yes*, I have been preoccupied with my mother's illness,*but* she needed me"; "*Yes*, I have focused on the kids, *but* they've got important exams coming up"; "*Yes*, I have been preoccupied *but* my work project is at a crucial stage" or even "*Yes*, we've had problems, *but* nobody's marriage is perfect."

Why this is a mistake: Your husband will feel either that you've not heard him or that you've not taken him seriously. Either way, it is a disaster. He will feel hurt, taken for granted, and probably switch off altogether. Alternatively, he will think, "If she won't listen to me, what hope is there of anything changing—so I'm better off leaving."

Talking about your love for him

He might not love you, but you're still desperately in love with him. There's nothing wrong with that. In fact, it's brilliant because it will give you the drive and determination to keep going through the dark times. The problem is telling him— again, and again, and again.

Why this is a mistake: When we say "I love you," we're half-expecting the other person to say "I love you too," "I love you even more," or "I'll love you until the stars fall from the sky." He knows what you want to hear, but you're just reminding him that he doesn't love you. Worse still, this strategy is making him feel depressed or a "bad" person for not returning your love. With each declaration, you're building a brick wall with your over-flowing love on one side and his empty heart on the other. I know this a big ask, but please, please, please don't mention the subject of love again until he brings it up.

Trying to convince him to stay

Splitting up is going to devastate the kids, you will have to sell your lovely house and you need to make him understand just how selfish he's being. Surely, it would be best to try and work on your relationship? You're also talking up how great your marriage is to balance out his bleakness. There is a lot of sense in this approach—that's what makes it a much better response than the previous two strategies, but it is also why it is particularly dangerous.

Why this is a mistake: There are three problems with this strategy. Firstly, he is talking from the heart (about his emotions, feelings, and heartache) and you're talking from the head (about facts, opinions, and beliefs). In effect, you're speaking two different languages. So you're bound to see things differently, disagree, and become angry with him. Worse still, your rational mind is telling you that if you present the facts one more time or marshal the evidence slightly differently, he will have to "see sense." So you try over and over again—which brings us to the second problem with this strategy. After so many discussions that either turn nasty or go around in circles, he will begin to believe that you're not supposed to be together because "we're such different people." In effect, not only does this strategy not work, but it provides him with more ammunition for leaving you. Finally, talking up good things about your marriage while he feels desperately unhappy will make him feel that you're not taking him seriously. And if you're not taking him seriously, nothing fundamental will change. So why stay?

Going for a quick fix

You're hurting so much, you think your heart is going to break. So of course, you want to feel better and right now. So you ask for reassurances that he can't give or you search for a magic solution. It might be getting away for a romantic weekend without the children or trying to seduce him with "knock your socks off" sex—after all, these are things he's always said that he wanted. Alternatively, you've backed down on all the long-term issues that exist between the two of you. For example, he can play golf as often as he wants. Although going for a quick fix might improve the general atmosphere in the house, or provide a couple of happy moments, the effect will not last for long. He will still be wary of you or determined to leave

Why this is a mistake: At best, he's going to think "she doesn't understand the depth of my despair" and, at worst, that "she thinks she can buy me off." Of course, he appreciates all your nice gestures, but he's also frightened that, once he's firmly back in the corral again, the bonus sex, free pass for fishing, or whatever, will be withdrawn and he'll be stuck in his miserable old life again. If you're being honest, you've most probably arranged great weekends away or tried harder before, but these haven't really changed anything beyond the short term. The other problem with a quick fix is that you become so focused on making it

17

happen that you're not listening to what he's saying and, when the quick fixes don't work, you're faced with the enormity of the struggle again. And that's the point at which you panic and undo all your good work.

Labeling him as the problem

You've been a supportive and loyal wife. He's got a lovely home and children who adore him. What more can he want? Of course, you're not perfect—who is? But you're not the one who is sending inappropriate texts to another woman, wanting to forget your responsibilities, or saying "I have to think about myself for a change." No, you're trying to hold the family together. If only he'd speak to someone and get help or simply grow up and start acting his age. In many ways, this is the most seductive option of the six unhelpful reactions to "I don't love you anymore." After all, you're looking beyond the surface and focusing on what could be driving his unhappiness. You're also trying to be supportive and caring by suggesting that he speaks to his doctor or consults a therapist.

Why this is a mistake: By labeling him as the problem, you're sidestepping your part in your marriage unraveling. One of my mantras—covered in full in *I Love You But I'm Not in Love with You*—is that problems are six of one and half a dozen of another. Of course, it might seem that your husband is the problem if he's been behaving badly recently. But what if you pull the focus back from this crisis to look, for example, at the last two years. How does that change the picture? Did he feel unappreciated, taken for granted, or second best? Please don't think that I'm trying to excuse him or blame you, but rather to help you imagine how he might be thinking.

The next problem with giving him a label—such as being depressed or going through a midlife crisis—is that it seems only sensible to find a solution. So far, so good. Unfortunately, it's easy to get sucked into the previous, unfortunate strategy and go for a quick fix or a magic solution. For example, if only he'd see the doctor and get some medication, everything would be fine and the whole family could breathe again. That's why you push, cajole, and beg him to make an appointment and, all the while that you think you're sorting stuff out, you're really putting more bricks into the wall between the two of you.

In the meantime, he just gets more angry, dismissive, or obstructive—even though you're trying to look out for him and getting more and more puzzled. Let me explain why. It's highly likely that you're giving him the message, however unintended, that "I'm OK, but you're not." When someone feels criticized, even lovingly, they get defensive, justify themselves, or go on the attack. The one thing criticism never achieves is to make someone feel more loving toward you!

In the most destructive versions of this strategy, you will not only label him as a deadbeat dad, but label yourself as the heroine. At this point, the situation will begin to polarize even further and instead of looking at what you need to change, all your attention focuses on changing him. No wonder you feel stuck and helpless! Ultimately, the only person we can change is ourselves (and you're in danger of shutting down that option).

I hate you: don't leave me

Nobody consciously decides to try this option, but it's where many women end up—particularly if they've been using the other failed strategies. In other words, you haven't really listened to your husband or, in your mind, have downgraded his pain. Meanwhile, you've talked up your love for him, in your attempts to convince him to stay, and fanned your emotions to almost unbelievable heights. In such moments, your everyday marriage becomes the love match of the century! No wonder you're in so much pain. No wonder you feel so rejected. No wonder your heart is about to burst.

At this point, you think "It's best to let it out," or perhaps you've been trying so hard to hold back that suddenly you're swept away on a wave of emotion. Out comes a flood of recriminations, frustration, anger, and perhaps even violence (toward yourself, him, or your joint possessions). A few minutes later, you're in tears, begging for forgiveness and promising never to do it again.

Why this is a mistake: Once you've stepped back and understood the pattern, it's easy to see why "I hate you: don't leave me" is a disaster. Not only are you giving him really mixed messages, but no man wants a scary wife. You might think that an apology allows you to start again but, in reality, every episode adds a truck-load of bricks to that wall between you. If you are at risk of tipping over into ranting and the "I hate you: don't leave me" state, please step away rather than further damaging your relationship.

Six best reactions to discovering your husband doesn't love you

I would be very surprised if you didn't make one of the mistakes I've outlined—probably more. But don't worry or get angry with yourself—that will change nothing. The important thing is to stop the unhelpful behavior and substitute it with as many of the following helpful strategies as possible.

Acknowledging

It is really simple. When he seems angry or sad, don't pretend that it hasn't happened or try to jolly him along. You say: "I can see you're angry with me" or, when he switches off, ask him, "Could you explain how I've hurt you, because I'd really like to know?" You fear that by acknowledging his pain (or other feelings) you will make things worse or perhaps that he'll say something you'd rather not hear. And you're right, in the short term, you will probably get an outburst of anger, frustration, or an unpleasant truth. However, you are showing that you're truly interested in all his emotions or opinions—and not just the nice or loving ones.

Don't worry if you can't pinpoint his feelings—for example if you say he is "miserable" when he felt despair. He will soon correct you. You can still use this strategy even if he doesn't seem to have any feelings—because that's also a recognizable emotional state. For example, "You're feeling distant, switched off, or detached." There is another type of acknowledgment and it sounds a bit weird or artificial, so many people dismiss it out of hand. What is it? You simply acknowledge what has been said (rather than identifying the feelings behind them) by repeating back his last sentence or the main points of his message. For example, "I didn't support your when you were really snowed under at work."

Why this works: Whether you are acknowledging his feelings or his words, you will make your husband feel that he is heard—rather than just "managed" or having lip service paid to his opinions. He may get angrier, sadder, or say something hurtful (because acknowledging feelings can temporarily bring them to the surface) but, firstly, it burns them out and, secondly, you've probably learned a bit more about what's going on in his head. So I can't say it often enough: acknowledge, acknowledge, and acknowledge again. If you are ever in doubt about what to do over the next few difficult weeks—just try to identify his feeling or repeat back the last part of his sentence. Even better, try both. For example, "You're feeling angry because I have neglected you."

Listening

I wouldn't be surprised if you've raised your eyebrows at this suggestion. You'd love to listen to him, but he won't open up or he's basically emotionally illiterate. Of course, I've counseled men who are on the autism scale (where their brains are wired differently to most people), but the vast majority are not only too willing to talk about their feelings but are grateful for the opportunity. So what stops them? Time and time again, women complain their husband is a closed book, but the minute that he starts to speak in my counseling room, she will interrupt or, worse still, tell him that it's not like that. And guess what? Men just clam up or think"what's the point?" Yes, lots of men haven't been trained to think about their emotions—just to get on with things. However, if you give your husband time and a bit of encouragement, he will tell you what he's thinking or feeling.

The other way that women shut down men, often unintentionally, is with tears or anger. Men hate to upset women. I know that sounds like a strange statement, considering what he's been up to lately, but please take it as red (I will explain more in the next chapter). So rather than risk upsetting you or making his life more difficult, he will simply appease or withdraw and hope for the best. In other words, he will keep the peace in the moment, even if it's storing up more trouble in the future.

The final reason men clam up is that they feel their wives are "cleverer" at arguing and will "twist" their words around, so they defend themselves by saying "I don't know" or "I'm fine."

Even if your husband is articulate, emotionally fluent, and good at arguing his case, it is still important to make him feel heard. After all, if you're interested in all his wants, needs, and opinions, you will be showing him that you're interested in him—rather than just his salary, having someone to share the load of running the house or because he's the father of your children.

So every time you feel tempted to speak—bite the inside of your cheek and nod your head instead. If you're doing something else at the time—however important—stop, turn around, and look at him. Even if he says something outrageous or makes an accusation, don't defend yourself, but acknowledge what he's said. For example, "You say I've been controlling" or "I keep overruling you about how to deal with our daughter." As a rule of thumb, I would bite the inside of your cheek or acknowledge what he's been saying at least three times before explaining yourself or responding to him.

Why this works: There are two advantages to this strategy. As you will probably have guessed by now, it will make him feel that you've taken him seriously, understood where he's coming from, and provided a glimmer of hope that things could be different. However, more importantly, you will get a better idea of what is making him unhappy, as well as see the beginnings of a way forward to save your marriage. This strategy is crucial. Basically, you can never do too much listening.

Check it out

This concept is basically acknowledging and listening—but ramped up. You don't just show him that you have heard him, but ask questions and get clarification. For example, "You're angry because I disagreed with you in front of the children. How did that make you feel?" He might reply "belittled" or "useless." Don't defend yourself or try to put the record straight; just ask another question. "Were there other times when I overruled you?" Good questions start with words such as Who, Why, What, When, Where, and How. For example, "What would you have liked me to do?," "When did this start?," or "Why was this so painful?"

It is important to double-check that you have heard correctly. This is because when he is saying something painful your mind will be racing, interpreting, and trying to find solutions. You may not only miss some vital piece of information, but may also jump to conclusions—possibly the wrong ones. For example, he might feel that you run him down in public. Before you dismiss this as banter with friends where you might poke fun at him (in a nice way of course), ask, "Could you give me any examples?" Perhaps he means that you contradict his opinions when you visit your parents (because lively debate is what happens in your family) but it makes him feel small.

Why this works: In many ways, saving your marriage is not about trying harder (unless you have completely taken him for granted or been totally preoccupied with the children), but being smarter and targeting your efforts. In other words, you are using your energy where it will really count. That's doubly helpful because smarter is not only more effective than running around in circles, and exhausting yourself by changing everything, but can be sustained over the long term. Another advantage of checking it out is that it will stop your mind spinning out of control (and panicking), because you will ask, "Did you say you have never loved me?" and he will clarify, "I have wondered if I truly loved you or whether it was an infatuation." I know these answers are both horrible, but there is a big difference between thinking something and believing it. Fortunately, checking it out allows you to register the difference, rather than exaggerating it and starting to panic again.

Imagine every word he says is true

The previous, positive strategies have been relatively straightforward, but this one is really tough. However, if you can pull it off, it is incredibly powerful. So how does it work? Forgive me if I state the obvious. We see the world through our own eyes and experience it through our own emotions. Our interpretation of an event will always be filtered through our own particular lens. However, someone else, who has an entirely different history, will have a different take. For example, what might seem like sorting out a pressing problem to you might be instigating a horrible row to your husband. It is very easy to get wedded to our own view of the world and to discount or downgrade everyone else's.

What's more, because we each have 100 percent access to our own motivations, what we do makes perfect sense to us. For example, "I don't mean to nag, but if he doesn't listen the first time what choice have I got?" Through this lens, it is easy to think "If he doesn't like it, why doesn't he pull his finger out?" So you "I'm tired and stressed," and you mentally add, "Aren't you always," and because—in your eyes—the job is incredibly important, you can downgrade his opinion that next weekend will be soon enough ("because it's not true") or dismiss it ("When have I heard that before?").

Instead of looking through your own eyes, I want you to put your interpretations to one side, remove all your justifications, explanations, and mental brackets, and imagine that what your husband says is the truth, the whole truth, and nothing but the truth—because in his eyes it absolutely is true.

So if every word he says is true, what would you like to change about your behavior? If his complaints or opinions still seem too far-fetched to be true, go back to checking it out, and ask more questions, such as "Could you give me another example?" When you truly understand his opinions, you're ready to move forward again.

Why this works: This approach is like sitting right next to your husband and being 100 percent on his side. As I've explained before, it not only gives you a fresh perspective, but also some important strategies for solving the crisis. However, there is also a hidden benefit to this strategy: if you give your husband the gift of imagining every word he says is true and really understanding him, he is more likely to pay you the same compliment and return the favor. If you're finding this hard and retreating into the "Yes, but..." response (for example, "He should take some responsibility for this problem" or "He's really hurt me"), please stop for a second. If you truly love him, doesn't he deserve the respect of imagining that, for him, what he says is true?

Processing

With these positive strategies, I have asked you to listen, acknowledge, ask questions, and ask even more questions. I have also encouraged you not to justify, explain, contradict, or try to find solutions. If you're about to explode with frustration, don't worry. You're about to get your opportunity to defend yourself.

So what is processing? Instead of giving a knee-jerk reaction to your husband's complaints, promising to change or going for the quick fix, I want you to sleep on what he's said or, at the very least, go away and think it through. Afterward, tell him the main conclusions that you've drawn from your conversation and what you plan to do to rectify the situation. When he's had a chance to correct your interpretation of his complaints and comment on your suggested remedies, you can report back about your feelings—for example, "I'm really upset that you think ..." or "I really love you and I want to make things better." Then you could give your side of the situation—for example, "I do want to make love to you, but I've been so tired lately."

Why this works: Not only have you listened, but you've also gone away, thought about what your husband has said, and discussed your conclusions with him. This is probably the opposite of what has happened in the past.

You may have reacted immediately because what he said—or didn't say—was hurtful: so you've appeased him, played the "poor me" card (tears or getting resentful), exploded with anger, or made a sarcastic comment. In effect, the conversation has been closed down. Alternatively, you've let it drop, but gone away and really thought about it. By this, I mean that you've taken his silences and the few facts that you've gleaned and churned them over and over in your mind, then come up with your own interpretations of his behavior. In his silence, it is easy to misconstrue several random comments or actions and for your opinions on his motivations to become the truth. This is what he means by "You've twisted what I've said." For example, he says, "I'm really busy at work," and in your overthinking of this snippet of information it's become, "He hasn't got time for his children" and therefore "He doesn't love them as much as I do." Perhaps you've tried to engage him in conversation but, really, you've just told him your conclusions and he's got angry, walked away, and, once again, any meaningful conversation has been closed down.

However, by processing, you are involving him and checking out your findings, rather than second-guessing and overthinking. Finally, you are ready to lay down the foundations for teamwork and the beginnings of a well-made plan for rescuing your relationship (more about this later in the book), rather than panicking and pushing him farther away.

Getting the right help

While most men don't have enough emotional support, many women have too much. In fact, my heart sinks when a new female client says, "My friends have been wonderful," because I normally have to listen not only to what she thinks is wrong with her marriage (which is helpful), but to her friends' views too (less helpful) and, in one case, even to her hairdresser's analysis! Yes, it can be useful to have an outside perspective (to stop thoughts going around and around in your head), but all too often it can slip into polling all your friends on what to do next. You may get confused from so much contradictory advice and also risk pumping up your distress ("You'll never guess what he's done now") and fanning the flames of overanalyzing ("What does it mean when he says, 'It's complicated?'"). Worse still, because your friends and family love you and want you to feel better, they favor quick fixes and magical solutions which, as I've explained, make matters worse, not better.

When you're considering who to tell, please think about the long-term implications. Off-loading all the gory details could make it hard for your husband to socialise with your friends and family in the future—especially if you have been blackening his character to them. Please, whatever you do, don't involve your children—particularly your daughters—if you suspect infidelity. I often work with couples where the wife has long since forgiven her husband for being unfaithful, but the teenage daughter is still angry with her father (and feels that he has cheated on her personally). It is also unfair to ask your children to take sides; undermining their relationship with their father will not help your relationship with him either.

Why this works: There will be times when you're feeling emotional and need a shoulder to cry on. It is far better to off-load to an understanding friend than to risk begging your husband for another chance or sounding off at him about some inconsiderate behavior—yet again. Friends will also help you to keep a sense of perspective—and stop you from taking all the blame. So how do you decide who would make a good confidant? Look for someone who will listen rather than advise. Ideally, she should have been through something similar and come out the other side and, if not still with her husband, at least be on good terms with him. If in doubt, ask yourself if she has her own agenda. Of course, it's fine to have two or three supporters, so there's still someone to talk to if your number-one confidant is out of town, and to consider therapy or consulting your doctor or priest.

Coping with your panic

It is all very well for me to stress the importance of keeping calm, listening, and processing everything your husband is saying, but what if every word pushes you farther over the edge?

> *"My husband hasn't wanted to discuss where we went wrong; he just says we're going over old ground. I am ashamed to say that I've handled everything wrong: pushing him constantly for answers as to why things went so wrong and what I did to make him stop loving me. Unfortunately, he would just say nothing and sit or stand there staring. It is like having a conversation with a brick wall and he decided to move out and get a six-month lease on an apartment.*

Against my better judgment, I consulted a solicitor friend, who advised that we would be better to divorce since that would give us a legally binding document. I presented him with this because it is what I thought he wanted, he was taken aback and just sort of shrugged off the divorce talk. I asked him that day if this could have been avoided had he spoken to me in the beginning about how he was feeling: he closed his eyes, looked in my direction, and nodded yes. He then proceeded to say that it couldn't be avoided now, could it?

If I am honest, I am scared to ask him anything else for fear of what his answer would be. I am generally scared of him at the moment, he just isn't the man I married and spent half my life with."

It is important that you recognize the first signs of panic or that everything is becoming too much—rather than doing something you will regret later. So what are the signs? It might be that your chest feels tight, a sinking feeling in the pit of your stomach, your breathing is getting faster and shallower, a splitting headache, or you just feel generally stressed. When your body is telling you that you can't cope, please use one of the following six strategies.

Concentrate on your breathing

If you are alone, put both hands flat against your diaphragm. (You will find it just under your ribs.) Feel your chest rising and sinking. Try to slow down your breathing and take deeper breaths. If you are with someone, and want to do something more discreet, focus on the air going in and out of your nostrils and breathe deeper and slower. Keep this up for five minutes or until you feel calmer.

Burn off some excess energy

If you're like a caged tiger and simply can't think straight or concentrate on your work, you need to get out of the house or the office and do some exercise. My favorite is going for a run, because I think fresh air and being away from your normal surroundings gives you a fresh perspective. You may prefer to go for a swim or take an aerobics class. The choice is yours. If childcare means that you can't go out, tackle some physically demanding job—like the kitchen floor or an overgrown flower bed in the garden.

Keep a diary or start a blog

It is much better to pour all your worries and thoughts into a diary than to burden your husband with every twist and turn of your private thoughts. Instead of letting a million and one questions go around and around your head, put them down on paper or on screen. This will distance you a little from your panic, and may produce answers from your ramblings. It is also helpful to return to your diary and reread it. With luck, you will discover that you're making progress and that, although today might be bleak, it's better than yesterday or two weeks ago.

Speak to just one of your supporters

You might think that if you just speak to your husband, he will reassure you that everything will be OK or that if you got a few answers about why he's so unhappy you both could move forward, but when you're panicking the conversation is unlikely to go well. So pick up the phone or send an email to your supporter: she can be a dumping ground for all your fears and help you to get everything back in proportion. For example, you probably wouldn't feel better if you had proof that he's having an affair or "If I forced the situation, then I'd have clarity and that's better than not knowing."

Plan for a better future

Instead of kicking yourself for what you've done wrong in the past, focus on what you need to do to make things better. At the moment, you might not have many ideas, but this book is full of them. So instead of panicking, start reading. There are simply hundreds of self-improvement or self-help titles. (You will find a recommended reading list at the back of this book.)

Step away

If you're in the middle of a discussion or an argument with your husband and you can feel yourself beginning to get angry (not just regular anger, which is OK, but the kind of rage where you say stuff you will regret later or start ranting), in danger of sobbing, begging him to stay, or pushing for "answers," please step away. Tell your husband, "I'm sorry, but I need a break," and leave the room. You could try out another of my other coping strategies and either return after ten minutes to half an hour, or text and tell him you're all right. Perhaps you'd like to continue the conversation at this point, make an appointment to talk at another time, or simply ask to drop the subject. There is no right or wrong approach, but please try avoid unhelpful behaviors that push him away.

Be kind to yourself

I will return to this theme over and over again: your husband falling out of love is one of the toughest challenges that you're ever going to face. You're going to make mistakes; after all, you're stressed, frightened, and probably not sleeping properly. Please, please, be kind to yourself. My guess is that you're doing really well, under very difficult circumstances. So look after yourself by eating well, cutting yourself some slack (in the greater scheme, it doesn't matter that the kitchen cupboards need tidying), and pampering yourself from time to time (have a long bath, buy a magazine, or go on a night out with the girls).

Love Coach's Three Key Things to Remember

- More relationships end because of a wife's panic than a husband's determination to leave.
- Listen to your husband: really listen to what he has to say.
- Think everything through before you act.

CHAPTER TWO

Why doesn't my husband love me anymore?

"My husband and I have been married a little over a year and been together ten years. We've always been very much in love. Six months ago, he told me he wasn't happy and wasn't sure if he still loved me. One of his complaints was that he didn't feel loved by me, and I didn't ever hug or kiss him—it was always him hugging or kissing me. I have listened to all of this and made a huge effort to hug him more often and show physical affection, but every time I've tried, it seems like he's pushing me away. Last week, he sent me a text message saying he couldn't carry on like this; that he has tried talking to me, but he couldn't. He said he knows I've been trying really hard, but he just doesn't feel the same. When I got home we talked again, but haven't resolved anything; he has just told me the same things again. He has now gone to stay at his parents' house. I'm frightened we're going to talk ourselves into divorce and, try as I might, I can't understand how we've got to here.?

You've probably begun to accept the idea that your husband doesn't love you. After all, his behavior and the atmosphere in the house makes it impossible to ignore the problems. But you simply can't get your head around "why?" It's not that long since he stood at the altar, or in front of the registrar, and all your family and friends and promised to love you for better or worse, richer or poorer, come what may. No wonder you keep asking yourself why. No wonder you get more and more frustrated when he can't give you a satisfactory answer. And even if he has given you a half-decent reason, for example "I don't feel appreciated" or "You don't listen to me," it doesn't explain why he wants to leave—especially after you've tried so hard to change.

Perhaps your answer to "why?" is that another woman has

turned his head and is poisoning his mind. You might be right. However, it doesn't explain how your marriage became so vulnerable to outside influences or why your husband felt so unloved that he was tempted. So we're back at why again.

Instead of plumping for easy or superficial answers, it is crucial to get to the root of the problem. Otherwise, you risk patching up your marriage and putting it back on the road only for it to crash a few years into the future (perhaps that's what you've already done). So my aim in this chapter is to look at all the layers underlying this crisis, because I think "why?" is a really important question and deserves a comprehensive answer.

Three things women need to know about men

There is a huge hole in the debate about relationships and how to make them better: men. I spent over twenty years working for Relate (the UK's leading couple counselling charity) and, for the majority of that time, I was the only man working at my center. When I went on training courses, I would put out the flags if there was one other man there. I'm in private practice now and share a building with probably thirty or more other therapists—and women still outnumber men by five to one.

If you read a debate in the newspapers or watch TV on topics that affect both men and women—such as parenting, pornography, sexually transmitted diseases, or divorce—time after time, it is women talking to women, with not one man involved. Of course, some women try to explain what men might be thinking or feeling, but others parade their prejudices or simply dismiss men's opinions as wrong. Sadly, men have either opted out of these debates or too few of us have looked deeply at our motivations, at who we are or what we need.

Therefore I'm not surprised that your husband can't explain himself (in a way that makes sense to you). It's not that he's necessarily being evasive or lying (which is often what women in my therapy office accuse men of doing); it's more likely that he doesn't have the words or any previous experience of looking deep into his soul. Meanwhile, you're also probably frustrated with yourself for not being able to get through to him or make any sense of what he does say. The result is that you're both stressed, in pain, and angry, which does nothing to help good communication.

So please be compassionate toward both your husband and yourself, because you're missing three vital pieces of information that most women don't necessarily know and most men don't know how to explain.

Men subcontract their emotional lives to women

Men are brought up to act, rather than to examine their feelings. The cliché that men don't "do" feelings is either accepted by both husbands and wives (who don't look at the implications) or challenged (because this generation is more emotionally literate and willing to discuss their feelings) and therefore they deny that there is a problem. However, even the most modern man and hands-on dad subcontracts much of the emotional running of his life to his wife. For example, she buys the presents (often even for his mom), she runs their social life (so he has to check with her if he's free to play soccer with his buddies), and she's lead parent (who knows the name of each child's current best friend, puts school sports day on the calendar, and reminds him to take time off). If he has a problem at work, she will help decode the office politics and advise on how best to handle people. If he falls out with their children, she will broker a peace deal or help to "explain" him to their rebellious teenager.

So it's not so much that men aren't in touch with their feelings, it's more that they have subcontracted them to women, who will interpret and explain them to him and, if there's a problem, alert him and send him off to see one of the army of women in the caring professions.

The implications: What happens if the person he has a problem with is his wife? In an ideal world, he would talk to her. But what if she feels attacked and either dismisses his issues or gets angry and shuts down the conversation—or perhaps he fears that's what would happen? That's why many men put their problems in a box and say, "It doesn't matter," or "It will get better when … the children go to school, we have more time on vacation, or the Chicago Cubs win the championship." To keep the lid firmly shut on his problems, a man has to switch off any feelings such as distress or anger. Unfortunately, you can't choose which feeling you switch off and, over time, you end up switching off every emotion—even the loving ones.

Although it's possible to struggle on for years living a half-life, there will be a crisis: all the lids come off the boxes and, of course, you know what happens next, because you're currently living with the consequences! Perhaps this is the cruellest part of all: because you're responsible for his feelings it's therefore your fault.

I think you can guess the implications of willingly (or unwittingly) taking on his feelings: when there's a problem, you feel blamed and a failure. (It goes without saying that this is deeply unfair. However much you care for your husband, he is an adult and you're not responsible for his feelings. Of course, you can help him over any obstacles in his path—that's part of the deal of love and marriage—but you shouldn't have to carry him through life.)

Men can't handle female anger

The bond between a mother and a son is extremely strong. For the first few years, she is usually the center of his world and it's not an exaggeration to say that she holds his well-being (and maybe his life) in her hands. If you have a son yourself, you'll know how much he wants to please you and how uncomfortable he gets when you're angry (because that seems to be the opposite of love). While a girl has to grow up and become like their mother, a boy has to please and keep his mother on his side (because she's still a powerful figure in his life who will intercede with his father, teachers, and so on). As he heads toward his teens, he has to leave the world of his mother and begins to identify more and more with his father. During this period, he looks to his father for a role model on how to deal with female power. If he's lucky, his mother and father will have an equal relationship where they can openly express their feelings or needs and, when they clash, know how to negotiate and find a compromise that is acceptable to both of them.

Unfortunately, lots of couples split power down the middle and although they achieve a sort of equality, she's in charge of the house (even if both parents work), their relationship (because men outsource their feelings to women), and the family—while he's in charge of everything else. However, boys spend the majority of their time in the domestic sphere and have no real understanding of work or money (and the power that comes from there). So what a boy sees are the disputes about chores, home improvements, and childcare and, more often than not, his father will either appease his mother, slide away when she gets angry, or agree to do something to her face and then go his own sweet way. What he is unlikely to witness is his father listening to his mother's anger; acknowledging when she has a fair case (and doing something about it); and, when necessary, standing up to her so she does not become "she who must be obeyed."

There are other reasons why men find female anger hard to handle. If a boy is angry with his male friends in the playground, they will fight and it's over and done with. However, if he falls out with his sister or a female classmate, it's really frowned upon "to hit a girl." So what does he do? How does he process his anger?

The implications: As I said in the last chapter, men want to please women. After all, they have subcontracted their feelings to them, so it's in their best interests to keep things nice. It's also why lots of men want a quiet life. Therefore, in order to avoid their wives' anger, many men will go along with what she wants (not always with the best of grace); allow his opinions about the children to be overruled (because he doesn't want a row, which he will probably lose); and, when things get nasty, either switch off or walk away and wait until her anger blows over.

Although these strategies work in the short term, they just make women angrier in the middle term; so the relationship enters into a downward spiral in which a husband's retreat into avoidance and his wife's righteous anger get worse and worse. Worse still, many men have a faulty internal thermostat, which measures the emotional temperature in the room. If his parents never expressed any anger or even mild disapproval, his wife's annoyance or frustration will register as rage or fury. Similarly, if they rowed all the time and he witnessed violence or name-calling, even a slight atmosphere could put him on red alert and he may interpret even a mild rebuke as a devastating criticism.

Fortunately, lots of women are only too aware that men don't respond well to anger or have seen how he tries to keep his mother sweet (whatever the cost). So she tries to curb her distress, to rise above her frustration and, in the words of many of my female clients, "have the patience of a saint." As I've already explained, it is impossible completely to suppress your feelings. After weeks of bottling up issues, feelings, and needs, you will explode with anger and he will go running for cover and blame you for causing the upset in the first place!

Don't worry, I'm not going to ask to ignore your anger, because that's counterproductive, but to report your feelings. I'll explain more about this in the next chapter (where we will start your fight back).

Men believe in love more than women do

I know this is a controversial statement. Especially as research shows that both men and women rate love as the most important ingredient for a successful relationship and it's women who read romantic novels and stop to watch a bride arrive at a church. So let me explain why men believe in love more than women do.

If you ask women about their tastes in books, movies, and so on, they will explain that it's just a bit of escapism away from the grind of everyday life. Certainly, when a woman has children she will not let "love" rule her life; she has bigger responsibilities and concerns. She is also more willing to hear the central message from all my books: love requires skills as well as connection (which I think is an optimistic idea, because skills can be learned or improved).

Meanwhile, men believe in love, as in the "All You Need is Love," "Ain't No Mountain High Enough," and "You Raise Me Up" sentiments of pop-song writers and poets. This is because men need to believe in the power of love. After all, if you've sub-contracted your emotions to someone, she had better have your best interests at heart. If you can't stand her anger or disapproval, she had better not only like but truly love you. In a nutshell, love is a man's insurance policy and the only way he can cope with the contradiction of handing a woman his heart for safekeeping while being terrified of being so vulnerable.

The implications: Although it is touching that men believe love can perform miracles, it can also make them reckless, blind, and—I'm sorry to say this—stupid. Even though a sensible part of every man knows that chatting up another woman will only lead to trouble, the attention makes him feel better (for a while) and, before long, he's talking about his problems (which is the beginning of subcontracting his feelings) and suddenly he's in love. In his mind it has to be love with a capital "L," rather than lust, because only love "can lift him up" (from the slough of despond) or "put him back together again" (and help his life make sense). So despite all the evidence of his eyes and the advice of his friends, he's torn between his wife and children and the other woman, who of course is never angry or full of recriminations. Meanwhile, his wife is trying to talk sense into him and dismiss his feelings for the other woman. However, when she attacks their "special love," he will naturally start to defend it and, in so doing, builds it up to almost epic proportions (with magical powers) because otherwise his problems would seem insurmountable.

Even if there is no other woman on the scene, in male logic, if you've been preoccupied with other stuff—like the pile of ironing on the landing or your kids' forthcoming exams—he will wonder if you truly love him. After all, "love will conquer all," "forge streams," be the "wind beneath your wings," and, who knows, cure cancer too. So if you're too tired to have sex, well, maybe you don't really love him.

I know this is depressing, but I think it is better to know just what you're up against, why it seems like you're talking to the wall, and to understand why this isn't going to be a quick fix. Even if you do need the information in Part Two of this book, understanding how his mind works is the first step to countering the negative influences of the other woman.

Three reasons why he might have fallen out of love

I have worked with around two thousand people over the past

thirty years. So although I don't know the exact reason why your marriage is in crisis, I have a pretty clear idea why most relationships hit the buffers. In my experience, it comes down to three factors. Many relationships can survive the first two reasons— probably for years on end. It is the third one which is fundamental and provides a theme to which I will return over and over again.

> *"My husband and I have been married for 26 years, together for 30 plus years; yes, childhood sweethearts I suppose. We have two wonderful kids, obviously all grown up now. I had the 'I love you, but …' speech last year. He said it was down to trust issues, the fact that I had been keeping things from him about the kids. Nothing major: I have lent them money to help them out and not told him. The relationship between my husband and our son was, at the time, very strained. I used to be monkey in the middle between them and it was painful to see and hear. My husband basically wanted me to report back to him every time our son did something wrong; the atmosphere was awful. I thought trying to smooth things over between the two of them would help their relationship."*

You put your children first

I know this is another controversial point. Of course you put your children first! If they're babies, they really are helpless and need you. Meanwhile, your husband is a grown-up and can sort himself out. After all, he loves his children dearly and wants the best for them too. So what's the problem? You're one hundred per cent right and I don't want to argue with you. However, babies grow up into children, who don't need us quite so much, and then students, who leave home and go off to university, but some mothers still drop everything for them. For example, I've had clients who have been willing to set off on a three-hour round trip to her daughter's college room to find her lost passport (because her daughter was too busy to look for herself); another had a copy of her daughter's reading list so she could help with her coursework. I know these are extraordinary examples, but I have many of them. Meanwhile, your husband is probably putting the children first too. It's only natural. However, in the process, many couples exhaust their marriages and end up being coparents rather than lovers. Whenever someone writes to me that they have "beautiful" or "wonderful" children, it sounds an alarm that the couple is probably putting the children at the center of their lives and neglecting each other.

Why this is so harmful: If you let each other slip down your list of priorities, you will both feel taken for granted. There will be times when you really need your partner's help, but the routine needs of the child have trumped yours. Meanwhile, it is easy to mistake happy family intimacy for couple intimacy and not realize just how lonely your husband might feel. If this sounds familiar, please read my book *I Love You But You Always Put Me Last: How to childproof your marriage*. I know you're going to want to say, "yes, but …"; however, it is possible to bring your husband up your priority list, and have more fun together, without harming your children. In fact, it's in their best interests too. Basically, if your husband believes that he is just the father of your children and someone to fetch and carry for them, he will not feel loved by you and will begin to detach (in order to protect himself from this depressing scenario). It won't be too long before he's fallen out of love.

Your sex life has lost its spark

There have been some massive strides since the sexual revolution of the sixties, particularly over the past thirty years in which I've been counseling couples. Everyone is more relaxed about talking about sex and women have been given more permission to enjoy sex, rather than simply doing it for men. Although there is much to celebrate, sex therapists, relationship counselors, and society in general have been so busy stressing that no one should be forced to have sex they don't want that we've forgotten the other half of the equation: no one should have to do without the sex they do want. Meanwhile, we might be getting better at talking about sex in general—certainly with our friends—but it is still hard to talk to our partner. If you were to ask him, "Do you fancy going somewhere different for our vacation this year?", you'd expect a spirited conversation and an internet search of possible destinations. If you were to say, "Do you fancy doing something different in bed?," he'd most probably reply, "What's wrong with our sex life?" and go into a sulk. In the worst-case scenario, he might even think you were having an affair! So although you don't listen to the same music, eat the same food, or go out to the same places that you did when you met, because it's almost impossible to discuss sex, you're probably doing the same things in bed. No wonder your lovemaking is more likely to be functional than passionate. Many couples I counsel are having sex as seldom as three or four times a year and others have not had intercourse for as long as seven years, but have never really discussed the impact on their relationship or tried to do anything about it.

Why this is so harmful: Sex bonds us to our partners—so we're not just coparents—and makes us feel happier in ourselves and more forgiving of our partner's irritating little habits. So why don't we do it more often? Alan Riley, Professor of Sexual Health at the University of Central Lancashire, has analyzed a large number of people and how often they fancy making love. He plotted a graph from those with the lowest amount of desire to those with the highest. The majority of the population, of course, lies somewhere in the middle. However, Professor Riley noted that women score on the lower end of sexual desire and men score on the higher end. So if you're a typical woman in a relationship with a typical man, you are probably going to want sex less often than your husband.

In an ideal world, the two of you would discuss frequency and negotiate a solution, but few couples are able to achieve this. What happens in the majority of cases is that the person who is least keen on sex—normally the woman—ends up being in charge and the frequency level settling somewhere around the point at which she feels comfortable.

Worse still, because women can "survive" longer without sex than men, they can often use sex as a bargaining tool. So lots of men complain to me that sex is used as a reward. Does your husband feel that if he's nice to you, dances through the hoops, and presses all the right buttons in the right way, that he maybe, just maybe, get lucky? Could he think you don't really enjoy sex or that you do it to keep him sweet? Even if this is not the case, if you seldom or never initiate lovemaking, he is not going to feel truly desired or that there is a spark, a real connection, in the bedroom. Here is the real problem in many modern marriages: while he uses sex to feel closer, you are likely to want sex only when you already feel close. No wonder sex can turn into a battlefield.

Fortunately, I have a program that deals with different levels of desire, helps couples talk about sex, and get the spark back. I explain it in my book *Have the Sex You Want: A couple's guide to getting back the spark*, as well as in an app with videos to guide you through my ten-week program. You can also find advice about sex and how it fits into your campaign to save your marriage in Chapter Four of this book.

Poor communication

At this point, it might seem that you're in a hole with no way out, but don't worry. The third, and most likely, reason for your husband falling out of love is also the foundation for your fight back. So why is communication so important? Despite the fairy tales and the myth of soul mates, it is impossible for two people to live happily ever after and in complete harmony without falling out from time to time. That's why you need to be able to sort out niggles before they fester into resentment and to negotiate when bigger conflicts arise, so your marriage does not fall into the trap where one of you wins and the other loses. Unfortunately, we are not taught about good communication at school and if your parents swallowed confrontation, one of them squashed the other or they fought like cat and dog, you won't have learned at home how to resolve problems either.

Why this is so harmful: On the surface, everything seems fine. Yes, there might be a few squabbles and sarcastic comments, but nothing to worry about. And that's the real danger. One partner—probably your husband—is feeling ignored, a second-class citizen in his own home. Meanwhile the other partner—probably you—remains in blissful ignorance; or if you are aware of issues, you don't think they are that serious.

It is impossible to ignore problems forever, so when the crisis does erupt it comes as a complete shock, not just to you but your friends and wider family too. Worse still, your husband could feel that it is "too late" and he's already tried to "solve the problems," but this normally involves trying to push the problems even farther away (and therefore this approach is doomed to failure). With poor communication, what would have been a difficult but fixable problem becomes impossible to resolve and therefore there's only one solution: to split up, tell the kids, and look for someone else.

What happens when you can't communicate properly?

Although you are 100 percent committed to saving your marriage, if you're being honest with yourself, you'll admit that there are areas of your relationship that need improving:

"Last year my 40-year-old husband of nine years (we've been together for $11\frac{1}{2}$ years) had a short-lived affair and then gave me the 'I love you, but …' speech. He is the most considerate husband at home, and we never had any disagreements related to household or finances because we both have difficulty expressing our needs and making clear how important things are. I am indeed difficult to argue with. I am stubborn and tend to come up with logical arguments to make my point. He ended up giving up instead of fighting for what he wanted (even though our discussions were always polite). An example: over the years he's expressed a wish for me to dress really feminine from time to time (skirts, high heels, stockings, etc.). I am not a natural with stockings and high heels, and I have big feet. He told me several times that guys are more visual. I cannot stop asking myself now why I did not give my best in fulfilling his wish? On the other hand, his lengthy computer games and TV-watching made me feel ignored and neglected. I understood that he needed his time with computer games as a way of dealing with pressure at work, but we

42

could never agree what would be a fair amount of time for him to devote to gaming."

When someone cannot resolve everyday problems or issues, they fall into one of the following traps.

Being passive

With this communication style, your opinions, needs, and wants are of no importance. So you will either deny them outright: "I don't care, you choose," or will prioritize your partner's needs over yours: "Of course, I'll clear out the attic if you think it's important" (even though you're exhausted and would much rather unwind than work your way through a list of chores). Relationships where one, or both, partners are suppressing their needs can be very happy—at least on the surface. There are certainly no arguments, but being a people-pleaser can have a terrible long-term cost. If you've always done what other people want, you can lose touch with your own needs (and wonder "who am I") or feel that you're loved only if you're "nice" or "agreeable" and do what other people expect (and therefore stop being your own person).

If this is your husband: He's a nice guy who will do anything for anybody. The children love him, but he's a bit of a pushover and your daughter, in particular, knows how to twist him around her little finger. It is perfectly possible for your husband to jog along for years in the passive role. Especially if making other people happy makes him happy. In effect, your husband has been trading any short-term benefits of getting his own way (for example, going fishing rather than visiting your parents) for the middle-term benefit of a harmonious household. However, over time, there are only so many times he can swallow his own needs without feeling he doesn't count and becoming disillusioned with his marriage.

If this is you: On the surface, going along with what your husband wants seems a great strategy. Who doesn't want to get their own way? Many marriages survive and even flourish where the man is in charge and the wife trots a couple of paces behind—especially if his mother "adored" him and gave him a sense of entitlement. However, it is only a short step from being compliant to being a doormat. Meanwhile, just doing what your husband wants in bed, rather than what you like, will not make you feel sexy and desired; slowly but surely all the passion will drain out of your lovemaking. There is also a danger that your husband will lose respect for you and think—there's no nice way to put this—that you're "boring." Sadly, it's human nature not to appreciate what we have and to long for what we don't have. In the worst-case scenario, he will be on the look out for a sparky, challenging relationship with an exciting and unpredictable lover.

If this is both of you: I sometimes come across relationships where both partners are passive and spend the majority of their time going along with what they think the other person wants. It is often a complete revelation when they both discover this: "But I thought you wanted to …," "No, I thought you wanted …." With these sorts of relationships, both partners will put the needs of the children first—because their interests are paramount—and neglect both their own interests and those of the marriage.

Being domineering

With this communication style, your opinions, needs and wants are extremely important and your partner's are of little or no importance (or more likely, you've never really stopped to think about them and have therefore downgraded or ignored them). Alternatively, you might have convinced yourself that your opinions are "right" and your partner is "wrong." So, of course, you need to organize a sleepover for your daughter's classmates (so she's not isolated from her year group) rather than having quality, couple time with your partner (because you can do that any time). Some people call this communication style "aggressive," because it can be achieved by shouting, getting angry or being sarcastic and putting down your partner (so they begin to believe that their opinions, needs, and wants are truly of no importance). However, I meet just as many people who get their own way without being overtly aggressive. They just do what they think is right and damn everybody else, for example, emailing arrangements for the weekend to their partner after they've been made and it's too late to change. They will then bribe their partner, "Let me have my own way and I'll give you sex"; sweet talk them around,"Pretty please"; or make them feel guilty, "You don't care about our daughter."

If this is your husband: I'm afraid that I'm going to make another sweeping generalization. Little boys are taught to win (sometimes at any costs), while little girls are taught to cooperate and be more sociable and therefore be more aware of other people's feelings. So you will try to go along with his wishes, but often there's a conflict between his needs and those of the children. Perhaps you think he's overly authoritarian and secretly sabotage what you consider his diktats and, for example, let your daughter go out in a short skirt. What often happens when men are domineering is that women will start an unofficial sex strike—although you won't necessarily have called it that—because "If he's not nice to me or ignored me the whole day, how can I suddenly turn myself on at night?." If this is you, when sex does happen, you're likely to be giving out the unspoken message: "Just get on with it." In many cases, you're getting your needs for intimacy and closeness met by giving your children a cuddle or having a long chat with your girlfriends. Although you are not particularly happy, you can jog along for years, especially while the children are small.

If this is you: If your husband has let you have your own way, no wonder you've been so happy and in love. Unfortunately, he hasn't got such a great deal himself. However, some random event, such as his morning train getting stuck for two hours because of a fatality on the line, may make him stop and question his whole life: "Why do I get up early, spend half my life commuting to a job I don't really like, come home late, and spend the weekend ferrying ungrateful kids about? There's got to be more to life than this?" You probably won't even have noticed or have just shrugged it off ("There are always delays") or he won't have said anything because he knows you'll have sensible answers, such as "We need the money." Maybe he's just not the introspective type. Sometimes, the trigger is a row, such as wanting a weekend away with his mates, but he feels overruled and talked over. Whatever the background, something has shifted inside and, in his mind, you've turned from loving into controlling. This will seem baffling to you, because you've only ever wanted what's best for the family.

However, he has been working on the unspoken deal, which he may not even have articulated to himself: "If I sacrifice my needs, she will really love me and therefore give me what I need." I know this is tough because if someone doesn't tell you that they're unhappy or stand up for what they need, how can you second-guess? Unfortunately, in his mind, by overruling, for example, the golf tournament (because his children never see him), you've broken the unspoken deal and he will never get what he truly wants.

If this is both of you: Your relationship is a set of battles to get control. You're regularly clashing and, although there is a lot of sound and fury, nothing ever gets resolved. Once again, something has happened, such as one of his parents dying, which makes him think "Life is too short to live like this" or "I've had enough." Perhaps there has been a shift in the balance of power—maybe he's lost his job or his business is in trouble—and he feels defeated and dejected.

Swinging between being passive and domineering

This communication style comes in two forms. Firstly, you alternate between being passive (and downplaying your opinions, needs, and wants) and being domineering (and downplaying your partner's opinions, needs, and wants). Often these approaches focus around specific parts of your life. For example, a woman may be domineering about a couple's social life, making plenty of time to see her friends, but little to see his, but be passive about how money is spent in the house, so she pays her salary into the joint account but he just transfers some money from his private account each month. Meanwhile, a man can be domineering, for example, about being allowed to flirt with other women at parties because "It's just a bit of fun," but be passive when it comes to issues about the children because "That's her domain." More frequently, a person will be passive most of the time and let their partner be in charge until something makes them snap. At that point, they become domineering and shout, browbeat, or sulk until they get their own way. More often than not, their partner is so shocked that they back down straight away, not because they think their partner has a good case but because they want to avoid a scene. This of course stores up future resentment.

The second form of this communication style combines being passive and domineering at the same time. The most common version is called passive aggressive. When someone is asked to do something, they immediately agree. So it seems, at least on the surface, that their needs, wants, and opinions are of little importance. However, underneath the pleasant exterior, they are seething because they do think that their needs, wants, and opinions are important. For example, a wife will ask her husband to redecorate the spare bedroom because her mother is coming to stay. He doesn't want to use his weekends on home improvement or want her mother to come and stay, but he doesn't tell her this. Instead, he agrees to do the work to her face, but then quietly sabotages it. He has to watch Major League Baseball on TV or he gets drunk on Saturday night and is too hungover to make a start on Sunday. The alternative version is domineering, but in a passive way. Once again the needs of the person asking is paramount, but they pretend to be passive. For example, they will play the martyr, "poor me," or make their partner feel guilty: "I do so much for you and all I ask is this one little thing."

If this is your husband: If he can't say no and uses passive-aggressive behavior to get his own way, it is very destructive. Often neither of you feels powerful: he will think you are in charge (because you set the agenda), while you will think he's in charge (because he's always digging his heels in and stopping you from getting things done). You will both be frustrated and angry and your relationship will feel like a constant battle.

47

If this is you: A lot of women pride themselves on being cleverer than their husbands: "I always get my own way because I make him feel it was all his idea" or "I can twist him around my little finger." However, deep down, I don't think they respect their husbands or, if they are being honest, really want to be so manipulative. It can also be exhausting having to manage your partner and there is a danger of feeling as if you've got an extra child to look after! If, however, you are being domineering but in a passive way (by whining, wheedling, and being tearful), this is equally frustrating for your husband and behaving like a little girl will make him lose respect for you.

If this is both of you: Lots of marriages work perfectly well where one partner is domineering in one sphere and passive in another. However when circumstances change, for example after the birth of a child or the children leave home, one of you gets promotion, or in the wake of an affair, the balance of power will shift and what seemed tolerable beforehand is no longer acceptable. If you are both swinging between being straightforwardly passive and domineering, you risk combining the worst of both communication styles.

What's the alternative?

Fortunately, you don't need to be passive, domineering, or a combination of both. The alternative is to be assertive. In this communication style, both parties' needs, wants, and beliefs are of equal importance. Each partner asks—rather than demands or manipulates—but also listens to their partner's requests. So how can you be assertive and still deal with disagreements or competing needs?

- Negotiate and find a middle way, for example "Let's go to the party, but leave early."

- Trade with each other, for example "I'll go to your party if you'll look after the children so I can go out with my friends next week."

- Concede one of you will back down, but only after feeling truly heard, because the other person's case is stronger. For example:

"Even though I hate your works' outings, going to the party is really important for your promotion prospects and I want to support you."

As you can see, assertive behavior avoids the traps of resentment, losing sight of your own needs or lessening your respect for your partner and the open and honest dialogue also allows you to solve day-to-day problems. More importantly, it raises the prospect of your marriage being truly different in the future. In the next chapter, I will explain more about being assertive.

Love Coach's Three Key Things to Remember

- Men consider women to be relationship experts and often unconsciously subcontract their feelings to them, then get angry when they don't make them happy.

- Most relationships deteriorate because of a variety of interlocking reasons.

- There is no one single magic bullet that will solve this crisis. However, better communication will lay the foundation for a better marriage.

CHAPTER THREE

Can I fix things on my own?

"My husband and I have been having problems for about nine months. I knew he wasn't happy and we had talked about it before, but one day he came home and told me his feelings for me had changed. He swears there is no one else. He asked for time and space, which I refused to give him and I begged him to stay and work things out. He did stay, but did very little to show that he cared enough to want to work it out. Now he is moving out. I am devastated. How could he do this to me and our two young children? He says he resents me and is angry with me. He says I was too much of a mother and not enough of a wife. We have not been intimate for about two months now. What can I do; is there any hope to save my marriage when I am the only one trying?"

By this point, you should have a clear idea about why your husband has stopped loving you. It might be something that he has complained about a million times but you have not really taken seriously before; the buildup of years of bad communication, which you have just diagnosed; or something that you had always known was a problem but hoped that ignoring it would make it go away. With a better understanding of what's gone wrong, you're ready to start crafting your strategy for saving your marriage.

Don't worry, if your husband is unsure, swinging back and forth between hope and despair or has even checked out of your marriage altogether, the first step of my recovery program needs only your commitment to change.

Making a fulsome apology

You have probably said that you are sorry a million times before. Worse still, no matter how much you have promised that things will be different, your apology has fallen on deaf ears. So I would not be surprised if you're feeling a bit skeptical. However, I doubt that you've made a fulsome apology. What's the difference? Well, "sorry" is something that trips off our tongues, sometimes when we don't mean it, but want to keep the peace. Meanwhile, a fulsome apology has the following elements:

- *It acknowledges your unhelpful behavior*. For example, "I have taken you for granted."

- *It accepts your responsibility*. For example, "I have been so bound up in looking after the children that I've forgotten to be a wife as well as a mother" or "I've been so wrapped up in my work that I haven't made our relationship enough of a priority."

- *It identifies how this situation has made your partner feel*. For example, "It has left you feeling alone, frustrated, and angry."

- *It expresses sorrow*. For example, "I'm really sorry for everything." You might even like to mention a particular instance that you regret. "Most of all, I regret that I got angry when you suggested spicing up our love life and bought those sex toys."

- *It explains why it won't happen again*. For example, "I'm going to arrange for us to have nights out together at least once a month." It is best to offer something specific that can be measured or checked off rather something general (such as "trying harder") that could mean one thing to you and another to your husband.

- *It is sincere*. Choose a time when you're calm and collected, rather than angry, resentful, or desperate, because that's how your apology will come across. Look your husband in the eye and check your body language is open (no crossed legs or leaning away from him).

Even when I explain the fulsome apology, some women are still unsure. Of course, they will give it a try—what have they got to lose? However, they don't really have any faith in it. If you fall into this camp, let's look at your reservations. It could be that you still don't "get" your husband's complaint. How could he resent you for trying your hardest and doing your best? If this is the case, you've probably apologized before and for a hundred other things, many of which you consider yourself "unfairly accused." If you are a people-pleaser, you might have spent half your life apologizing! However, I'm looking for something different. I want you to truly mean this apology. If that is hard, I'd like you go back to "Imagine every word he says is true" (see page 23). If you still find the apology sticks in your throat, please don't make it. Find something else that you do regret and for which you do wish to apologize. Men are not stupid. They know when they are being appeased; after all, you've done it before and all it has done has put off this evil day. For a genuine fight back, it has to be an apology that you will stand by and follow through.

Perhaps you are doubtful about making a fulsome apology because your husband "already knows all that." On one level, you could be right, but he will still long to hear the words spoken out loud, because it demonstrates that you accept his needs are reasonable and acknowledges his feelings. As I've already explained, you can't acknowledge too often. Perhaps, in the past, you've also lessened the impact of an apology by adding a justification or shared the blame around to lessen your personal responsibility. You might have added the plea, "so why can't we try again?" It's a perfectly valid question, but it is likely to get your husband's back up and raise the possibility that you're saying this only to win him back.

So think through your fulsome apology and write down something for every heading before you speak to your husband. To recap:

- *Acknowledge unhelpful behavior.*
- *Accept responsibility.*
- *Identify how this made your partner feel.*
- *Express sorrow.*
- *Explain why it won't happen again.*

Finally, I cannot stress too strongly that you must be confident you can deliver any changes, rather than promise something unrealistic out of blind panic, such as "I won't invite my mother to the house again" or "I'll get the children in bed by seven on the dot." Could you really cast your mother out into the cold—however much she has undermined your husband—and what about bedtimes during school vacations, scout nights, or when the grandparents visit?

What if he doesn't respond or is just dismissive?

When you've made your fulsome apology, my advice is to give your husband a chance to reply but, unless he is particularly keen to talk, to walk away, and avoid tipping over into begging, pleading or other unhelpful behaviors which could undermine your good work. Anyway, it will probably take a while for everything you've said to him to sink in. And if you're the sort of woman who never admits to your mistakes—beyond the vague generalization "I'm not perfect"—he could be in shock! Alternatively, he might be the sort of man that needs to digest what you've said before he responds. Whatever the response, please don't despair. You should see him softening over the next few days as he reflects on what you've said and once you've had a chance to deliver your promised, different behavior.

Hopefully, your husband will accept your fulsome apology as this will draw a line in the sand between the past and the future, but if he doesn't, it will be because of one of the following reasons:

- He fears it will excuse your bad behavior.

- You might do it again.

- You don't deserve to be forgiven.

- He can only forgive you if certain conditions are met.

Although it is helpful to explain that you're not looking to excuse your past behavior, I wouldn't get into a debate, reason with him, or try to prove why he's wrong. Instead, I would use his skepticism to redouble your resolve to prove that you won't do it again, that you deserve to be forgiven and that you will strive to meet any reasonable conditions for being forgiven. In this way, you will keep strong and develop resilience which will be vital for the journey ahead.

How do I recruit my husband?

You've recovered from the shock of discovering your husband doesn't love you anymore, you've begun to understand why and made a fulsome apology. But how do you begin to fix things, especially if your husband is uncooperative or thinks it's too late? No wonder many women despair and ask me, "Doesn't it take two people to make a relationship?" So let me give you the good news. It might take two people to make things work in the long term, but one person can get the ball rolling, initiate change, and ultimately recruit the other to save the marriage.

If you've tried to save your marriage, but got little thanks and loads of hostility, you might still be doubtful. What might have gone wrong? Unfortunately, the most common strategies for "working on a relationship" are fine under normal circumstances, but these are not normal circumstances. At best, they will get your husband's back up but, more likely and much worse, turn you into the enemy.

Five strategies that you think will work, but probably won't

You've probably tried one or all of these strategies, because they've turned your relationship around in the past or because your family or friends have suggested them. There is nothing wrong with any of these strategies, in moderation. Unfortunately, when they haven't worked, you've decided the problem was not trying hard enough. So guess what? You've pushed harder and harder and met more and more resistance. You've not only exhausted and depressed yourself, but made your husband despair. So what are the five strategies that normally repair a relationship, but are unlikely to work at the moment?

Being especially nice

You've been cooking his favorite meals, keeping the children off

55

his back, telling him how much you appreciate him, and offering sex whenever he wants it. In fact, you've been doing everything he's always said he wanted, but he still doesn't love you.

Why you think it will work: If one of you doesn't try to lighten the mood, you will both become seriously depressed. What's more, you've seen the error of your ways and you want to start putting things right.

Why it doesn't work: Your husband will have noticed the changes and he will be torn in half. On one hand, he will want to smile at your jokes or soften to your loving gestures. On the other hand, he will fear that you can't keep up this behavior and, over time, everything will revert to normal and he'll be in the same situation again—only older and with less hair. Don't forget, he's in terrible pain and he wants it to stop. That's why the exit door seems very appealing but trying again seems only mildly tempting—because he can't risk getting his hopes up, only to find himself in the same place in eighteen months' time. For some men, your gestures will be too little, too late, or attempts to buy him off, especially if you've been trying so hard, for so long that you've become resentful. In addition, your moods are probably all over the place: super-nice one minute, withdrawn the next, then biting his head off and quickly apologizing. At worst, he won't know what to expect when he comes home and who wants to live like that?

Using the children

Of course you don't want him to be unhappy, but there are some things that are more important than our own needs, such as family and, most of all, children. In fact, he's being really selfish and shouldn't you point this out? If you have older children, don't they have a right to know what's going on and have a say in the family's future?

Why you think it will work: He says he loves his children and wants the best for them. So surely it would be best for them to be brought up by both their mother and their father. You've read some research somewhere that children from broken homes do worse at school, are more likely to take drugs, and end up in jail. So if he won't give you another chance, doesn't he owe it to the kids to at least try? If you're close to one of your children, perhaps your daughter, surely if she pleads your case her father is bound to listen.

Why it doesn't work: Your husband doesn't need to be reminded how high the stakes are. He dreads the idea of being a Saturday dad, dragging his kids around windswept zoos, and stuffing them full of junk food to assuage his guilt. He wants to read them a bedtime story and give them a goodnight kiss. That's why he has been ignoring his unhappiness for years. What's more, he's going to hear your concern for the kids as proof that you're interested him as a father rather than as a partner. And, let's face it, if he suggested that you were a housekeeper and nursemaid for his children and nothing else, would you jump at his offer? I know you keep telling him that you love him but, in his mind, you're probably not backing up your words with actions.

The other problem with this strategy is that you risk frightening yourself: "The children will be scarred for life" or "He's bound to get remarried and they'll have a wicked stepmother." I've even had a woman in my office wailing that she will "lose" her child. Closer questioning revealed that social services were not about to pounce and her husband was not poised to kidnap their son and take him abroad. She meant that she would have to go out to work and not be able to spend so much time with him. Such catastrophizing will not bring your husband "to his senses," but will make you panic or lash out with your tongue, thereby undoing all your good work on saving your marriage.

Finally, involving your children in your private disputes will open up any fault lines in your family and cause the long-term problems that you wish to avoid. You also risk becoming the wife of every man's nightmares: "She's turning my kids against me." Yes, he might stay because you've held a gun to his head or maybe he'll just say, "What else have I got to lose?" and leave. Either way, you will not only be losing out, but setting up a bitter and protracted divorce too.

Having long talks

Since your husband has told you that he's no longer in love with you, the two of you have talked about little more than "your situation," how he's feeling today, whether there's any hope, and what can be done to change things.

Why you think it will work: Everybody knows that you can't solve a problem without sitting down and talking about it. Certainly ignoring the problem isn't going to make it go away. And wasn't that how you got into this mess in the first place?

Why it doesn't work: Good communication is at the heart of a good marriage, but going around and around in circles isn't good communication. Constantly asking him about his feelings and cross-examining him about whether any of your efforts have changed anything is like digging up a seed to see if it has germinated! Worse still, these long talks suck any remaining fun and spontaneity out of your marriage. No wonder he wants to leave. Anything for a quiet life.

Trying to work out what he's really feeling

How can you solve this crisis if you don't understand his feelings or motivation? If he won't tell you or just cries, "I don't know," shouldn't you look through the clues, analyze what he has said, and come to your own conclusion?

Why you think it will work: Interpreting your husband is what you've always done. You've had years of reading the signs and you know him pretty well by now.

Why it doesn't work: In theory this strategy should work, and that's what makes it really tempting, but there are two fundamental problems with it.

Firstly, it has worked in normal circumstances because your guesses have been reasonably benign. For example, he didn't pick up your dry cleaning because he's had a lot on his plate. Except these are not normal circumstances—the future of your relationship is at stake—and you're coming up with completely negative interpretations. For example, he didn't pick up the dry cleaning because he's selfish, doesn't love you enough to consider your feelings, or perhaps he did it deliberately to spite you. Instead of attributing his motivation to something temporary or trifling, for example his mind was elsewhere, you view it as something fundamental or fixed, such as his attitude or character. No wonder you're so angry with him and he's running away.

Secondly, there is a fine line between putting yourself into his shoes—what I'm trying to help you do—and overanalyzing. What's the difference? In overanalyzing, you have failed to apply the rules of Ockham's Razor.

William of Ockham was a thirteenth-century English monk, who laid down a law of logic so powerful that it is still at the heart of problem-solving today. He urged philosophers to use "parsimony, economy, and succinctness" and to choose the solution with the fewest assumptions possible. In other words, the simplest explanation is usually the correct one. When you unpick the conclusions of overthinking—normally the result of hours of multiple interpretations—you will have a range of assumptions, often taken from different parts of your husband's life, which have been bolted together.

Ultimately, it is better to ask, and take his answers at face value, than to overanalyze and then tell him what he's feeling—that really gets men's backs up. It could quite easily be that he really doesn't know why, because he's been trained not to examine his feelings and just to act, or that he's behaving badly because he's frightened and lashing out at whoever is closest—normally you and sometimes himself. If you're still in doubt, look at your own motivations and feelings. I bet they can change a hundred times in just one day. Your husband is probably going through something similar. So please don't put his actions down to one unchanging factor.

Suppressing your issues with the relationship

You've been doing your best to keep the show on the road (if only for the sake of the children). Even if he's bitten your head off—perhaps the house was a mess because there wasn't time to tidy after your kids' play date—and you've smiled sweetly but said nothing. On a bigger scale, while he's gone on at length about what needs to be different (if there is to be any chance of salvaging anything), you've kept quiet about what's been making you unhappy. After all, you will do anything to save your relationship.

> *Why you think it will work: He's got enough issues to keep an army of counselors busy for the next 20 years, so you don't want to add yours to the pile. And won't it just confirm his fears that your marriage is past saving?*

Why it doesn't work: Walking on eggshells just makes your husband irritated or snappy. When you back down—even in the face of unreasonable behavior—he loses all respect. Worse still, he knows you're repressing stuff (which puts him on edge since he's not certain whether your mood is a reaction to his temper or something bigger) and you don't come across as "real." On a deeper level, he knows that you will not do just anything to save your relationship. For example, you won't agree to let him take another lover! In effect, he can't reason with "I'll do anything"—because instead of a sensible dialogue you're hiding behind this blanket statement. By contrast, if there are things that you want to be different too, it shows you have a real stake in changing your marriage for the better—rather than simply appeasing your husband. In other words, you become an equal partner in fixing your marriage, rather someone on your knees, begging.

Five strategies that probably will work

Once again, don't worry if you've fallen into one or more of the common mistakes while trying to save your marriage; it goes with the territory.

> *"The constant arguing and going around in circles due to my persistent questioning has resulted in us separating for "time out" in the last week, so that we can try and get a clearer perspective on things. We are going to counseling, and my husband hopes desperately that he can feel "that way" about me again, because he*

doesn't want to split up—but fears it may be inevitable because he "just wants to be happy." We have looked at all the other reasons that he could be unhappy, but he is definitely unhappy with me. I don't know how long I can put myself through the hurt of being with someone who isn't in love with me, but he is insistent that we give it some more time as he thinks it is too soon to make a decision. My problem is this: how can I stop myself from pressing the "eject" button, and what should I be doing to help improve the situation? I love my husband very much, and don't want to split up, but I get so scared of getting my hopes up only to be hurt again that I worry I will become a self-fulfilling prophecy."

Hopefully, you're beginning to understand what's gone wrong and are feeling a little more optimistic and ready to roll up your sleeves. Good. It's time to lay the foundations for winning back your husband.

Don't wait to recruit your husband

Instead of waiting for your husband to agree that the marriage can be saved, not to be so negative or to give some encouragement, imagine that he is 100 percent on board. For a moment, imagine the sense of relief and joy. Your heart will have stopped racing and a huge weight will have been lifted off your shoulders. However, if you are honest, you'll also be aware that this is only the beginning of the journey. A lot of work still needs be done to turn this relationship around. Think for a second: what would you like to change about your behavior? Write down these goals as this will underline your determination to follow through. For example: "I'm going to make an effort to greet him when he comes home," "I'm going to prioritize sex more," or "I'll think before I lash out with my tongue." Now you need to act as if your husband is committed to saving your marriage and to start putting your plan into action.

Why this will work: Time and again, couples get stuck because both are waiting for a sign from the other, so they can change, or reassurance, so they don't risk getting hurt, but that leaves each partner in a very passive position—waiting for their other half. However, imagining that your husband is onboard or has shown that he has feelings will free you from this trap and allow you to get to work.

Take the pressure off

If your ways of trying to save your relationship have simply pushed your husband away or, in his words, "done his head in," it is time to acknowledge everything you regret and identify the impact of your behavior on him. For example: "'I know that I have been trying to make you feel guilty and that's just made you angry," or "I've been wearing you down with constant questions and that's made you exasperated." Next, and most importantly, make a commitment to stop. For example: "I'm no longer going to beg," or "I accept that you don't know why you've fallen out of love." Finally, explain your commitment to change and lay out your manifesto: "Although I'm no longer going to … (for example: 'ask for a second chance'), it doesn't mean that I don't think we can sort this out. However, I'm aware that pressurizing you doesn't work. Instead of just talking about change, I'm going to show you how much I can change (or how things could be different). In the meantime, I'm not going to instigate further conversations about us, but that doesn't mean I'm not willing to talk, if you'd like to, in the future."

Why this will work: Taking the pressure off will not only improve the atmosphere in the house, but will allow things to return to something more normal. What's more, by explaining your behavior, your intentions, and inviting further conversations—on his terms—you have taken an important step to more open and honest communication.

Flip around your flop behavior

When we're stressed and anxious, we tend to respond in the same old way. For example, we get angry, go silent, or avoid confrontation. Although you know your default reaction doesn't work—because you've tried it a million times before—you can't stop yourself from doing it yet again. Perhaps you hope that by reacting bigger (shouting louder, sulking longer, or moving to another city) one more time, it will change the situation. Maybe you're not sure how else to react. That's the beauty of the flip/flop strategy: flip around your flop behavior. Ultimately, it doesn't matter how you act differently, because anything is better than the same old, same old—you know where that leads. So why not try doing the opposite? If you get angry, try being calm. If you clam up, try explaining how you're feeling. If you avoid confrontation, look at the section on assertiveness (later in this chapter).

Why this will work: By breaking out of old habits, you will have opened up the possibility of a different outcome. Even if your alternative approach doesn't work, it has shown your husband that you can change and it will provide hope for the future.

Learn to speak his love language

There are five ways of showing how much you love your husband. These are "Caring actions" (for example, picking him up from the bar after a drinking session with his buddies); "Affectionate physical contact" (for example, snuggling up while you watch TV together); "Appreciative words" (for example, "Thank you for cutting the grass at my mother's while she was ill"); "Creating quality time together" (for example, arranging a babysitter so the two of you can go out); or "Present giving" (for example, "I bought these mints because I know you like to suck them on long car journeys."). Unfortunately, we tend to express our love in the way that we'd like to receive it. So you might be showering him with appreciative words—because that's what you need right now—but he doesn't really hear your love because his love language takes the form of caring actions.

Why this will work: It will channel your energy into the love language that is most effective for winning back your husband, so you're not worn out, resentful, and wondering why nothing you do or say makes any difference. (For more about love languages, read my book *I Love You But I'm Not in Love with You*.)

Model the behavior that you'd like to see from him

When you're hurt or upset, it is very easy to take your frustration out on your husband. You justify it to yourself because "What can he expect if he does …?" or "If he hadn't done x, I wouldn't have done y." Unfortunately, your "bad" behavior will spark something equally unpleasant from your husband and, before long, you're caught in a negative spiral and matching each other, dig for dig, in a race to the bottom. However, there is an alternative. If you've got children, do you ever ask them to be the "big one" when they fall out with their friends or each other and to put aside their hurt and make peace? One kind or concil-iatory gesture sparks another one and, before too long, you have a positive, upward spiral. So why not try being calm, pleasant, and giving your husband the benefit of the doubt? For example, when he comes home late without phoning, think it is because he has been overwhelmed with work and he is really tired, rather than that he doesn't want to be at home. The first inter-pretation would make you warm and welcoming and the second cold and angry.

Why this will work: This is a concrete way to take responsibility and kick-start change in your relationship. More importantly, it will encourage your husband to be generous too and to start to give you the benefit of the doubt as well.

How being assertive can turn around your relationship

I'm now going to unveil the big gun that's going to save your marriage. However, it won't come as a big surprise, because I've flagged it up time and time again. Whatever the reasons why your husband has fallen out of love and whatever mistakes you've made trying to win him back, the key to transforming your relationship is improving day-to-day communication. Here's an example of the difference it can make:

> "I don't want to give up on the marriage as my husband is now more assertive and is starting to open up with his feelings (I have

always pushed for this, but obviously in the wrong way before) and I am the person he wanted me to be. I am trying to be less controlling, more willing to listen, and share responsibility (money has been mentioned as an issue as he felt he could never have any money from our joint account but he now has his own account again). I am happy being this person at last and feel quite comfortable with myself—I wish I had done it sooner as I like me now! However, he still checks with me that he is doing it right, which I feel stems back to him worrying I will get cross with him if he gets it wrong (I used to do this in the past)."

Although good communication is the big gun for winning back your husband, no opportunity is too small for you to practice being different. In fact, everyday squabbles are the best place to start because the stakes are much smaller.

The assertiveness rights

Instead of your wants, needs, or beliefs or those of your partner taking precedence, with assertiveness, you both have equal rights:

1. To hold and express your own opinions.

2. To refuse requests without feeling guilty.

3. To set your own priorities and goals.

4. To judge your own behavior, thoughts, and emotions.

5. To take responsibility for the consequences.

So how does this work in practice? Assertiveness is all about being open and honest rather than hiding your feelings, but it is also about respecting the other person and taking account of what it might be like to hear your message. With this is in mind, I would suggest the following:

- *Think ahead.* Be clear about what you are trying to achieve.

- *Say something positive about your partner or the situation.* For example: "I know you have been trying hard," or "We seem to have been getting on much better."

- *Be specific and direct*. For example: "I would like us to go to our son's school concert together, even though we are separated." Do this rather than going for global goals, for example "I want us to do more as a family," which are hard to measure and could mean something different to your husband than they do to you. For example, he might think you expect him home earlier from work when you're talking about weekend activities.

- *Choose your timing*. Don't tackle an issue just as your partner is about to go out the door, but conversely don't bottle up your feelings until they explode into tears or anger.

- *Check your body language*. Look your husband in the eye. Aim for an upright and relaxed posture with your arms by your side (rather than crossed).

- *Avoid unassertive words*. For example: "I wonder if ..." or "Would it be possible ..." (such terms betray your lack of confidence and almost invite a refusal).

- *Stick to the facts and avoid judgments*. For example: "Most of the other fathers will be there," rather than "It makes me feel so unwanted."

- *Be prepared to negotiate*. Remember your husband has the right to say no. However, if he doesn't explain, ask about his reservations rather than backing down straight away. Perhaps if you had a greater understanding of his position, you could change your request to something that he could accept. For example: returning to the example of the event at the school, the husband might agree to come to the concert if there was no pressure to come back to the house or to stay after the children have gone to bed.

If your husband is passive

You might already have tried to get your husband to communicate more, but he just shrugs his shoulders or says "I don't know." Perhaps he had a domineering mother and his natural response is to go along with what powerful women want. Alternatively, he might be so used to considering everybody else's needs that he hasn't the faintest idea what he needs himself.

At this point, you're probably going to throw your hands in the air or even start to despair: "How can I teach my husband to be assertive? Especially as he thinks the relationship is doomed and is not going to want to read some book." Please don't panic. You're responsible only for your half of communication.

However, if you change and become assertive (rather than domineering), it will have a knock-on effect on how your husband communicates. I'm going to show you how to improve your listening skills, which will help him be more forthcoming.

Draw him out

Nod your head encouragingly, repeat back the last thing he said and ask questions. Anything that will give him time to think and delve deeper into how he feels.

Why this works: Since he was a little boy, your husband has been trained to act rather than feel. He might even have been given explicit messages such as "big boys don't cry," "put up or shut up," or "There's no use crying over spilled milk." His natural response will be to get out of this uncomfortable situation as soon as possible, but by drawing him out you will help him to start to listen to his own emotions.

Hold back your opinions

When there is an everyday problem with the children or a clash of family priorities, instead of giving your solution—even though you've probably already come up with one—ask your husband for his opinion. Then, instead of pointing out the holes in his thinking, ask more questions, such as "How will that work?"

Why this works: I once did some training for a company in Africa, but ended up learning just as much from them as they did from me. They had a saying in Ghana: "The big man speaks last." This is because once the most senior person gives his opinion, all debate is shut down. When it comes to family matters, you are probably the "lead" parent and your partner the "helper." In which case, your expert opinion makes you the "big man," so hold back and give your husband a chance to speak (and possibly fail) and to be taken seriously. In this way, you can form a team and therefore both be assertive.

Double-check

Instead of just assuming that he is on board with a plan, check, and check again: "Are you sure you can clear the shed this weekend?" or "Wouldn't you rather do something else?" This is especially important when he seems in a bad mood for no apparent reason.

Why this works: Instead of you taking his silence or half-hearted interest as agreement, he gains a second opportunity to tell you what's really on his mind.

Look at his body language

Are your husband's shoulders slumped or his eyes downcast? Does he have his arms crossed or his back to you? Is he mumbling so that you can't quite catch what he's said? These are all signs that he feels hard done by, downtrodden or is having trouble standing up for himself. So ask him calmly, "What does that sigh mean?" or "Why did you just shrug your shoulders?"

Why this works: When there is a mismatch between his lips saying "I'm fine" or "Don't worry about me" and what his body language is telling you, it's normally a sign that he's really struggling to be assertive.

Give him permission to say no

Sometimes people need support to say no. So tell him you won't be upset if he disagrees or wants to do something else: "It's not that important, so if you'd rather not ...," "I'd prefer you to tell me what you're really thinking," or simply "Are you sure?"

Why this works: In my estimation, about half the times that a man says "I don't know," he does know but is frightened of the reaction. So tell him, "I'd rather know what you really think," or

"I won't get angry." If your husband is a people-pleaser, he's going to worry about letting people down and therefore not being a good person. Giving him permission to say no offers him reassurance that you would rather have the truth than too easy an agreement.

Give him notice

Bring up contentious issues as early as possible, so your husband has a chance to think through all the angles. For example, if you're going to have a packed weekend when he wants to unwind, don't tell him at the last minute, when it's harder to cancel anything, but raise it as soon as you know it might be happening.

Why this works: It forces you to be assertive too, rather than sneaking unwelcome news past him at the last minute, and also offers both of you time to talk everything through, negotiate, and find a solution that works for both of you.

Praise him

I'm not talking about telling him that he's a wonderful father or a sensitive lover—not that there's anything wrong with such compliments—but look for ways to praise and encourage any assertive behavior. For example: "Thank you for telling me that you were unhappy that I stepped in while you were sorting out our son's homework," or "It really helped knowing you were angry, because I went away and had a long think about it."

Why this works: We all need positive feedback and this strategy reinforces change and makes it easier for your husband to be assertive in the future. Most importantly of all, it has shown that his greatest fear—"I will get my head bitten off"—is groundless.

If your husband is domineering

I'm not going to pretend that it is easy to communicate with an aggressive, angry, or domineering man. Maybe he isn't intimidating, but gets his own way through sulking or sarcastic comments and making everybody miserable until you back down to keep the peace. Alternatively, he might act unilaterally—buying the car he "needs" even though the family budget is stretched to breaking point—so that you're left dealing with a fait accompli.

Choose your ground

I'm not suggesting picking a fight, but next time you feel unfairly criticized stand up for yourself. Remember you have just as much right to your opinion as he does to his. Make it something small and specific and act straight away.

Why it works: It makes your husband stop, think, and be aware of how his behavior impacts on other people. Speaking up also brings all the conflict out into the open where it can be dealt with. Better still, you have chosen the battleground (where you have a strong case) rather than being ambushed (where you probably won't). If you feel overwhelmed by the force of his personality, tell him "I can't deal with five issues at the same time," or "Could I just respond to what you're saying?" Remember, you have an equal right to be heard and that includes equal time to argue your case, or at least to respond to his.

Acknowledge his anger or bad mood

You won't be surprised by this next strategy as it fits into my theme of acknowledge, acknowledge, and acknowledge again. Rather than trying to distract him ("Would you like a cup of coffee"), rationalize away his anger ("I know the kids have been difficult"), or solve his problem on the spot ("Why don't I go out and come in again"), just listen, and acknowledge: "So you're feeling angry ..." Follow up with questions, such as why has this made him so angry and how could we do things differently.

Why it works: Although you will probably get another blast of anger ("Of course I'm bloody angry because you're always running after the kids"), when a feeling is expressed it will burn itself out. It's only when it is pushed underground or converted into toxic thoughts, for example "She doesn't care about me," that they solidify into a concrete wall around your husband's heart. By staying with the conflict, rather than physically or emotionally running away, you will find out what's behind his anger—it might be something different from what you assumed—and he will feel heard. Even better, by acknowledging his feelings, you are a step away from acknowledging your own and standing up for yourself.

Criticize his behavior, not his personality

Nobody likes to be criticized, but if you've upset your partner, it is easier to hear that if it is about something you've done, or not done, rather than your entire personality. For example, if you say that you're disappointed that he didn't get home to bathe the children, he might be upset, but he will listen and with luck take on board your message.

Why it works: Criticizing his personality invites him to defend himself. For example, if you tell him he's thoughtless, he will get defensive and list every thoughtful action of his from the last five years. Alternatively, he will go on the attack and point out all your failings. By contrast, criticizing a particular behavior—preferably just after it happens—confines the argument to one specific incident, which should be reasonably easy to resolve.

Look to make a trade

With many couples, one partner is domineering in one sphere of the relationship and the other is domineering in another. (The most common split is for the woman to lay down the law in the home and the man about the needs of his career—even if both partners work.) Instead of alternating between winning and losing, negotiate a solution that benefits everybody—a win/win scenario. The easiest way to achieve this goal is to trade something you want from your husband for something he wants from you. For example, he will agree to stop dunking his toast in his coffee if you'll clear your paperwork from beside the family's computer.

Why it works: This strategy is particularly effective if you get stuck cross-complaining, when he moans about one thing and you retaliate about another. Moreover, if there's something in it for both of you, the agreements are more likely to stick.

Broken record technique

If your husband steamrollers over you, refuses to listen, changes the subject, or dismisses your point of view, repeat it and maybe repeat it again. Imagine a broken record where a needle gets stuck or a dirty CD. This is a very powerful intervention and should be used sparingly for really important issues.

Why it works: Not only does it stop you from becoming side-tracked, but also keeps you in the argument for that crucial bit longer. Time and again, in my counseling room, couples resolve issues, rather than one partner just backing down, because I encourage the quieter and less assertive partner to stand firm. If this strategy sounds rude, it can be softened, by alternating acknowledgments of your husband's opinion or feelings with repeating your point.

Don't push things under the carpet

What drives your husband's bad moods more than anything else is his feeling that he is not being truly heard. So the worst thing you can say is "Calm down," or "Let's not make a drama out of it," because this will seem as if you are denying his feelings or you are not interested. Unfortunately, he is probably right: you are uncomfortable with his negative feelings and have, in the past, tried to push them under the carpet. So be aware that even mild strategies to contain him, such as changing the subject or making a joke, could be heard as ignoring his feelings. Your husband has been programed to expect "Please take those nasty feelings away," or "I can't cope when you're like this." So he is either unaware or unconvinced of your desire to change and may hear a denial of his emotions even when one isn't meant. So how do you get around this problem? Yes, you've guessed it! Acknowledge, acknowledge, acknowledge: "I can see you're angry," or "Why are you angry?"

Why it works: If you ignore your husband's distress, it will seem to him that you are denying his opinions or that his feelings are not valid. Remember, your goal is to help your husband to switch back on his feelings and that means letting out all the negative ones too. Don't worry though, the positive ones—love, respect, desire—will follow. Better still, if you can accept his darker emotions as well as the lighter ones, he will feel that you can accept the real him.

Assertiveness in a nutshell

If you want a quick reminder, being assertive boils down to one sentence: I can ask, you can say no, and we can negotiate. It sounds incredibly simple, but we find it hard to ask for what we need (so instead drop hints, expect someone to know, manipulate, or simply demand) and difficult to say no (in case our partner won't like us anymore). Also, negotiating is a skill that takes time to learn and, before reaching a mutually satisfying conclusion, we have to deal with conflict and uncertainty without throwing in our cards or kicking over the table. However, if you can start to ask, be able to say no (or maybe), and negotiate, you will have the foundation for a relationship based on respect, equality, and love.

Love Coach's Three Key Things to Remember

- By apologizing for your mistakes, you will show your husband that you understand his unhappiness and have committed to changing yourself and the relationship for the better.

- The center of your fight-back plan is to be assertive, rather than passive or domineering. So don't swallow your needs, wants and opinions and don't expect your husband to do the same either.

- Even if your husband is not willing to cooperate on saving your marriage, it does not stop you from working on your half of the communication.

CHAPTER FOUR

How can I approach things differently?

"I have been with my fiancé for two and a half years. For the first two years, we were long-distance and he spends a lot of time away (because he is a marine). Recently, I found out he met a woman and had lunch with her. I caught him as soon as it started. From there, I questioned him and threatened to call every strange number on his phone. I then found out that he had slept with numerous women over the two years that I had waited for him and been faithful.

He apologized and cried and begged my forgiveness. My issue was that he had never seemed like he missed me when he came home. He didn't ignore me, but he didn't act like a man who had spent months away from the love of his life either. Our sex life was just OK. He had issues getting an erection sometimes and I noticed it more. After I learned of the cheating, I became hyper-sexual, needing the closeness and intimacy. It felt wrong because he didn't deserve the sex, but I needed it. It was amazing for a while and then he stopped being able to perform. This became a source of anger for me. I felt that he was not attracted to me and that is why he cheated. I felt so ugly around him.

In the past few months, he has been very cold when I have vented about how I feel and how he's not trying as hard as he should to make things up to me. Instead of understanding how I feel, he gets defensive and lashes out at me, saying hurtful things and treating me like he doesn't care. After hours of arguing and crying, he then will soften and tell me that he does love me and does think I am beautiful and just wants all the fighting to end. I feel like I am losing my mind."

Time and time again, I find couples are blocked from working on their marriages because of women's anger and men's inability to cope with it. In the worst cases, the men shut down, brand their wives as "crazy" and move on; as you can imagine, this fills their ex with rage and sets the scene for a nasty divorce and endless battles over the children. In most men, I find a fine balance between hope (that it can be sorted) and fear (she will never truly forgive me and I'll be sitting on a powder keg for the rest of my life). Therefore, it goes without saying, dealing with anger is a vital part of my plan to save your marriage. Don't worry, I'm not going to ask you to become a saint. I also think your husband should learn to cope with your righteous anger. However, the process should be fair—not about something that is outside his control—and at an appropriate level—not all guns blazing and taking no prisoners.

What about my anger?

There is nothing wrong with being angry. It's a natural human emotion and a clue that something is amiss and needs attention. Research from the Colorado State University found there was no difference in how men and women experience anger: the strength of their feelings and how much it is focused inward by bottling it up, or outward by becoming verbally or even physically aggressive. However, they found a marked difference in the context in which anger is expressed. Men are more likely to flip outside their relationship—hence all the public brawling and incidents of aggressive driving—and less likely to express their anger at home. Conversely, women are less likely to get angry outside the relationship, but more likely to "let it out" to their partner. Unfortunately, as men find it easier to calm themselves in marital disputes, they naturally expect women to do the same. Bearing in mind that men find women's anger difficult in the first place, it is easy for husbands to reach a nasty conclusion: "If she loved me, she wouldn't get so angry with me. Therefore, she doesn't love me and my life would be better out of this relationship."

Notice your anger

Most people explode because they've been ignoring all the minor things that upset them. That's why I want you to do the opposite for the next seven days and be really aware of *when* you get angry, *why,* and *what* you do. I'm not asking you to act differently at this stage, just to observe your anger and ask yourself the following questions:

- What happens when I hold in my anger?

- How does it affect the way in which I see the world?

- How does this affect my husband and my relationship with him?

- Does my anger create unnecessary trouble or pain for myself?

- How does it affect my self-esteem and my overall opinion of myself?

Look at the bigger picture

At the end of the week, go back over the reasons why you became angry. What are the patterns? If there are recurring themes, make a note of them—this is probably a clue that certain areas of your life need attention. Before I explain how to communicate your anger, I would like you to look at the bigger picture and ask yourself:

- *Is my anger fair?* For example, if your husband has a high-powered job (with a lot of stress) he might not want to go out to the theater (to see a play that doesn't really interest him) or rush out of the office to catch the exhibition that you booked months ago (and get behind with an important project). After all, you could go with a girlfriend and spend your shared leisure time with your husband doing something that you both enjoy. Alternatively, does it matter that he prefers, for example, a relaxed barbecue to a formal dinner party?

- *Have I asked for what I need or have I expected him to read my mind?* According to the angry letter at the beginning of this chapter (see page 75), the correspondent had wanted her fiancé to "act like a man who had spent months away from the love of his life." However, I doubt she had told him this or explained what behavior would have fulfilled her requirements.

- *Am I expecting something beyond my husband's pay scale?* By this

I mean, are you asking almost impossible tasks or ones that his upbringing or training make him ill-equipped to perform? Staying with the letter, the correspondent needs her fiancé to make her feel beautiful—and combat a culture that pores over the "flaws" of famous women and a multibillion dollar beauty industry dedicated to making women feel inadequate. Meanwhile, she is asking for a therapist's ability to listen to painful feelings and be empathetic. However, her fiancé is a marine, who is trained to do the complete opposite! Finally, we have to take responsibility for our own self-esteem.

- *Am I angry on someone else's behalf?* Many of my clients fall into a nasty trap where the fathers are underinvolved in their children's lives, beyond those as providers, and the mothers are overinvolved. Time and time again, women tell me that they have to protect their children. In many cases, this will be from perceived shortcomings in their husbands. If this sounds familiar, imagine what would happen if you allowed your older children to fight their own battles? Could they learn to express themselves in an assertive manner, rather than expect you to dominate on their behalf? In addition, do you risk becoming angry about something that your children are actually quite relaxed about?

- *Have I taken on too much?* Many women have such a tight schedule and have put so many demands on themselves both at work or at home—or allowed them to be piled on—that they have to run on 98 percent efficiency all the time. It only takes the dog to need to be taken to the vet and construction work downtown for the whole, complicated heap of responsibilities to collapse; then your daughter is half an hour late for her piano lesson. And when you're tired and stressed, it is easy to take it out on the nearest person—your husband—or to feel unappreciated by him (despite him not really wanting a dog and you having pushed for your daughter to learn the piano). Worse still, if you are a perfectionist and expect high standards for yourself, you could easily translate this expectation onto your husband and get angry about something, such as folding towels with the logo showing, that makes no sense to him.

Report your feelings

If your husband has done something that merits your anger, it is important to express it. Otherwise, there is a danger that it will turn into resentment and you can contain only so much resentment before it bursts out, in something ugly, divisive, and ultimately harmful for your relationship. Furthermore, anger can be really positive. It focuses our attention on something that isn't working and creates a sense of urgency to find a solution. So getting angry is OK. I just ask for it to be timely and properly expressed.

Let's start with timely. By this I mean that you speak up at the time or as close to it as possible, rather than six months later when your husband can't do anything about it. The more issues that you hold on to, the more they get tied together and harder to resolve. It might be possible to find a compromise about where to go for a weekend break, but not if you're also arguing about whether it's time for replacement windows and the pros and cons of separate bank accounts.

So how should you express your anger? I would like you to report it, rather than act it out. Let's start by explaining what I mean by reporting. Try using this format:

- I feel ...

- when you ...

- because ...

For example: "*I feel* annoyed *when you* come home late without calling *because* I don't know when to eat." The advantage of this formula is that simply naming the emotion will reduce its intensity. It also lets your husband know that you are "annoyed," rather than angry or even furious, which he might have suspected. "*I feel ...*" also owns the feeling, rather than "You make me feel ...," which puts the blame on your partner and raises the temperature so he doesn't hear the next bit. "*When you ...*" attaches the emotion to a particular behavior, rather to than your husband's character or everything he does. It limits the criticism to something specific and therefore manageable and fixable. Finally, *"because ..."* explains why. Otherwise, he could think you want to know where he is because you're checking up on him or want to control him, rather than looking forward to unwinding together over a home-cooked meal.

Next, let me explain "acting out." This refers to all the ways in which unexpressed anger, or other negative emotions, leak out. It could be slamming doors, huffing and puffing, nitpicking, sarcastic comments, sulking, playing the martyr, throwing a tantrum. If you're in any doubt, think of typical teenage behavior.

No angry texting or emailing

I can't tell you how often an entire session in my counseling room is taken up by a row over texts or emails. From time to time, the clients insist on me reading their exchanges—and they are full of random capitalizations (which seem like shouting), multiple swear words, insults, and threats. The problem is not just how horrible it is to receive such a communication—my heart feels like it is full of lead and I'm not even personally involved, but that it is permanent, available to be reread (and so bolster the feeling of being hard done by), or to be forwarded to other people (and so harden the lines of your support). Worse still, it could be accidentally read by your children. Something meant as a joke, maybe to lighten the mood, cannot be judged in that light without the context of facial expression, tone of voice, and body language. To compound the effect, most angry emails come across as rants and raise about half a dozen issues at once; as I've explained previously, the more topics, the harder it is to find a resolution.

So if you're going through a crisis and that's why you're reading my book, please follow the golden rule for texts and emails: think of them as postcards. Write only what you'd be happy for anybody else to read. Texts and emails are for communicating facts, such as "I should be home at 7p.m."; asking for details, such as "What have we got planned for next weekend?"; paying compliments, like "'I'm thinking about you"; or saying sorry. They are definitely not for resolving tricky or emotional disputes.

If you must text or email emotional material, report your feelings using the "I feel … when you … because …" formula, and keep the subject matter down to just one topic, rather than dumping half a dozen points and adding a PS.

There is more advice on managing difficult feelings in Chapter Ten, "How can I keep sane in an insane situation?"

What about nagging?

My hope is that overall communication will improve by helping you to express what's been bothering you in a less destructive way. However, it is equally important to stop a habit that could be destroying your relationship: nagging.

"My husband told me 'I love you, but I'm not in love with you' after a whole year of being very cold, withdrawn and distant. I was pregnant when he changed his behavior toward me, so at first I suspected it was a reaction to becoming a father for the second time or possibly some form of midlife crisis as he was turning 40 that year. I was also a bit too preoccupied with myself and my unborn baby (working full time and looking after a toddler) to realize how serious the problem was and to start doing something about it. On the few occasions that I asked or even begged him to explain his cold behavior, he only admitted that I had ground him down through years of nagging and moaning and that very often he had to walk on eggshells around me."

You've tried asking nicely. You've tried reminding when nothing happens, so the only way to get anything done is to drop pointed hints, criticize, or lose your temper. Not only do you dislike this version of yourself, but nagging creates an atmosphere in which your partner feels justified to countercomplain, start nagging himself or, worse still, believe your relationship is past repair. Fortunately, there are six strategies to get things done without resorting to nagging and pushing your husband farther away.

When you're in a hole, stop digging

You've tried a variety of ways to get your partner's cooperation. Common sense would suggest that if they haven't worked, you'd stop and try something else. Unfortunately, most people keep up with the same failed strategy in the hope that doing it bigger, louder, or just one more time will provide the breakthrough. Sadly, they just dig themselves into a bigger hole. So for an experiment, stop nagging and see how the atmosphere in the house changes. OK, you'll probably still be doing the lion's share around the house, or the majority of the childcare, but your husband will become more receptive to change—and the rest of the ideas explained in this section—rather than just digging in his heels.

Why it works: Not only does it create goodwill, but you'll also discover how hard it is to change for yourself (there'll be many times when you'll be about to nag, but have to bite your tongue). This will help you understand how difficult it will be for your partner to break his unhelpful habits too.

Make a fulsome apology

You've probably apologized before for nagging, biting his head off, or not thanking him when he did finally get off the couch. However, there is a difference between saying sorry, often to make up or keep the peace, and a fulsome apology. As I explained earlier (see pages 51–54), a fulsome apology identifies what in particular has gone wrong and how it impacts on the other person and includes an undertaking not to do it again. For example: "I'm sorry that I've kept on at you about clearing out the garage. It must make you feel constantly criticized. I promise not to nag again and if you catch me doing it again please say something." Although it is tempting to add an explanation ("I needed the garage cleaned out so there would be room to store my apple chutney"), it can sound as if you're excusing yourself and therefore lessens the power of your apology. There is sometimes an added bonus: your honesty might encourage him to own up to his nagging too.

Why it works: Admitting your mistakes will get his attention and an apology allows you to start again.

Reset the default

Most women nag because, deep down, they feel the division of labor in the house is unfair, especially if both partners are working full-time. Sometimes, it might seem quicker just to do things yourself, but that maintains you as the font of all knowledge— when your daughter does gym and the name of your son's teacher—with you "in charge" and your partner just doing you a "favor." So instead of constant trench warfare over getting him to "help out," for example, with folding the clean laundry, aim for a peace treaty where he takes over certain tasks. Chose a neutral time, not after a row, and talk through all the contentious areas. It normally helps if you agree to change something he finds annoying in return, because agreements stick if there's something in it for both of you. Finally, leave him to get on with his tasks and do them to his satisfaction, and in his timescale (within reason). Otherwise you risk perpetuating the "master and unpaid servant" dynamic which makes nagging so toxic.

Why it works: It makes cooperation something inherent, rather something he has to be reminded to do.

Offer alternatives

The reason we nag has its roots in our childhood. When we're small, we don't have the vocabulary or skills to negotiate and our parents hold all the power. Therefore, we're reduced to wearing them down, throwing a tantrum, or simply pestering, which are the three main components of nagging. With this in mind, I'm going to share a tip on gaining cooperation from toddlers which works equally well with adults. Basically, we all hate being told what to do, so we rebel or put up a show of defiance. Instead of commanding, offer two alternative outcomes, both of which are acceptable to you. For example, with a child holding something precious or delicate, you'd say, "Would you like to give that to me or put it back yourself?" With an adult who for example prefers to stay in rather than go out, instead of complaining about being bored, try asking, "Would you rather go around our friends' house tonight or to the movie theater on our own?"

Why it works: Instead of setting up a battle of wills with a winner and a loser, you can both win. He has the final choice of activity, but you've got your night out.

Praise what you do like

Most men are happy to do their share, but get demotivated because they feel constantly criticized. For example, they will get the children ready for school, make the packed lunch, put out all the right sports equipment, but the only comment they get is that they forgot to cut the grapes in half. Unfortunately, we're better at communicating the negatives than positives. And when we do notice, praise tends to be general, such as "thank you" or "that was helpful," or so over the top ("you're the best father in the world") that it doesn't seem believable. Instead try something I call "Descriptive Praise," when you give detailed feedback about what went well: "You put together a really balanced lunch for our daughter" or "I really appreciated it when you backed me up over our son's homework." This technique is particularly useful when you praise the steps toward big goals. So instead of complaining that the bathroom still isn't finished, tell him how much you admire the smooth finish to the grouting; it will make him feel appreciated and motivated to follow through.

Why it works: You can't make someone do something, you can only gain their cooperation. To this end, carrots work better than sticks. (There is more about Descriptive Praise in my book *I Love You But You Always Put Me Last: How to childproof your marriage*.)

Aim for more fun together

Lots of couples end up having a relationship that is all about getting things done and raising kids. However, life should be about enjoyment too. Although it is nice to have large projects to look forward to—perhaps a show and a meal afterward or a weekend break—it is equally important to play together. By this, I mean sharing jokes, silliness, flirting, loving words, and small surprises, such as baking him a cake or sending a sexy text. After all, you decided to become a couple because you had fun dating and doing things together. Why stop once you're married? And if you like each other, you're much more willing to do things to make each other happy.

Why it works: Couples who play together stay together and when problems occur they are attributed to the particular circumstances rather than a fundamental flaw in the relationship. Fun is also a building block for the next topic.

What about sex?

We all know sex makes us feel desired, closer to our partner, and a little more forgiving of his or her irritating little habits. Except, when you're busy and tired, it's easy to let sex drop down your "to-do" list and to fail to notice the impact on your relationship:

"After 14 years married and two small children, my husband (just turned 40) came to me pretty much asking for a divorce. We have always been each others' best friends and seemingly always wanted the same out of life. What we have always lacked was the physical and therefore the emotional connection that is truly needed to have a healthy marriage. He had always been the one to try to improve our physical/emotional connection, but with little help from me. I have always been a person with very high walls. He says he always knew this, but thought they would come down.

After the shock, I did a lot of soul searching and my walls and defenses came down. I realized why I had been that way (my Mom died in my early teen years) and how destructive this had been to him and me. In these last months, he and I have discussed all of this and he says he truly believes I get it, but fears that it is too late. He can't seem to gain the desire to try again or get past the fact that it took this long. He has a lot of anger about that. The confusing part for me though is that we have been more physically and emotionally intimate these last months than we have been in years, but it's still not enough. After any of these tender moments, which he says are very real for him, he feels anger, sadness, and emptiness. He doesn't feel the connection he wants to feel and this scares and makes him reluctant to share again."

As I've already explained, sex is really important to men. If your sex life has lost its spark, you've used sex as a reward, or its slipped down your list of priorities, your husband will think you don't really fancy him and, if affectionate touch is your husband's main love language, he'll also believe that you don't love him.

Once women realize that men consider sex as central to their marriage, their identity, and their self-esteem, they often ramp up their own sexuality, offer sex almost on demand, and explore activities that previously would have made them blush. On one hand, I applaud their bravery and commitment to saving their marriage. On the other hand, I worry that it could be counter-productive. So why should this be? Firstly, your husband will enjoy the sex, but worry that your lovemaking will eventually subside (in the same way that you changed from rampant while trying for a baby to less interested or even disinterested once you'd achieved your goal). Secondly, I want you to feel comfort-able with this frequency and type of sex. Otherwise there is a danger of becoming resentful and that will seep out through your body language or by being generally snappy. Most importantly, I want you to be assertive in everything, including your lovemak-ing. In other words, your husband's need for sex to feel close and your need to feel cherished before you're ready to make love are equally important. Finally, you need a sex life that is sustainable rather than a quick fix.

For all these reasons, my plan for saving your marriage centers on maximizing the feel-good effects from having sex and help-ing you to feel like lovers even when you're not making love.

Prolong the glow of lovemaking

All the sex manuals concentrate on foreplay, but I think after-play is equally important; by this I mean kissing, cuddling, and looking into his eyes for a minute or so after making love. You can further encourage closeness with a little affectionate pillow talk and telling him what you particularly enjoyed. It will not only make your husband feel ten feet tall, but encourage more of the same next time. If he tends to roll over and go to sleep, explain how much you used to enjoy after-play when you first got together and reassure him that you're asking only for a short time—even thirty seconds would be enough.

Create a connection by flirting

Although it's standard when we're courting, once we've settled down, flirting often goes out of the window. Sadly, lots of established couples are unsure what it involves or even how to do it. So let me explain. Flirting is giving your partner a bundle of sexual energy and seeing if he returns it—hopefully with interest. It involves in-jokes, gentle teasing, saucy texts, and reveals something about your heart. It also says 'I'm still attracted to you' or, if done at a distance, "I'm thinking of you even though we're apart," and builds up sexual tension—otherwise when you are finally alone together it's like trying to go from nought to ninety in a couple of seconds. Remember, flirting should be fun and playful—and it's only fun if both of you enjoy the joke and not playful if it could be interpreted as a demand for sex.

Romance starts outside the bedroom door

This is all about showing your partner that you care, but the power of romance is increased by novelty, otherwise it just becomes a duty. Therefore it needs to be renewed by finding different ways to express it and adding an element of surprise. It could be something sensual, for example having a bath together, washing each other's hair, giving each other a massage, or building a camp fire and staring into the flames. Another way is to add a new dimension to the ordinary, for example meeting up for lunch on a weekday, leaving a chocolate on his pillow, or both of you dressing smartly even though you're staying in. Other ideas include giving small presents or funny cards and expressing gratitude for something that could easily be taken for granted.

Aim for regular physical connection

This is perhaps the most important ingredient for increasing the general sensuality of your relationship and makes it easy to cross from the everyday world of paying bills, chores, and raising a family into the intimate world of sex. For example, kiss in the morning before leaving and in the evening when you return home from work. Lie in each other's arms on the couch as you watch TV. Encourage him to guide you through a door with a light touch in the small of your back or put your arm through his as you walk down the street. Otherwise you are in danger of falling into the "all or nothing" trap where any touch is an invitation for sex, rather than a chance to feel connected.

Act like lovers

Rather than turning into flatmates or coparents, use sexy pet names, sleep naked together, brush your teeth after meals so you're always ready for a passionate kiss, and arrange an occasional night out or romantic weekend away together. In a survey by the University of Colorado Boulder, which looked into frequency of couple's lovemaking, three quarters of parents had never taken a vacation away without their children. In a separate study at Harvard University, researchers found couples in love spend 75 percent of their time looking at each other when they are talking, as opposed to the usual 30–60 percent. So rather than shouting up the stairs, go and speak to him face to face and, when he's talking to you, turn around and put down what you're doing.

Make every session memorable

Sex becomes boring or a chore when you know exactly what's coming next. So mix things up and experiment. For example, there are lots of different ways of kissing—butterfly kisses (light and barely touching) and French kisses (long and lingering)—and different places on the body to kiss. Instead of focusing on the lips, try his neck and shoulders. Tease him by heading southward and then coming back up to the lips and starting again. You can also change the pace of your lovemaking by slowing down or stopping and making him beg for more and then speeding up again. Wake up your senses by playing romantic music, feeding each other with tasty tidbits, or wearing a favorite perfume.

Recreate that just-met feeling

See your partner through other people's eyes by going to his place of work and taking him out for a drink. Alternatively, invite him to your conference to hear you give a talk. Anything that allows you to take a step back and see each other as desirable and interesting people again, rather than possessions. Sex needs separation, as well as closeness, because we don't tend to desire what we already have. You'll also find a small amount of jealousy does no harm to your sex life whatsoever.

Don't expect mind reading

You're not the same people you were when you first met. You don't go to the same places or eat the same food, but lots of people still have the same sex. So update each other by sharing a fantasy—perhaps from a romantic novel or movie—rather than settling for the same old rut. It's equally important not to assume that you can read his mind too. So ask him questions—just like you used to when you were dating. Warm up with easier, general questions, for example "If you could live anywhere in the world, where would it be?," and move onto sexy ones, for example, "What one thing do you think would improve our sex life?" or "If you could make love somewhere you'd never done it before, where would it be?"

Love Coach's Three Key Things to Remember

- If your husband thinks that you spend the majority of your time complaining, nagging, or getting angry, he will feel that all the joy has been sucked out of your relationship.

- Every interaction with your husband—however small and even if you're separated—is a chance to try out the skills you're learning.

- Focus on creating a sustainable sex life, which places lovemaking at the center of your relationship.

CHAPTER FIVE

How can I keep strong when I'm getting no encouragement from my husband?

"I have discovered that I've been a very unhappy and insecure person for a number of years. I had not realized the affect that my unhappiness was having on me, my partner, or my relationship. As hard as the past eight months have been—I still cry almost every day—I am thankful to my husband for leaving as I feel this really gave me the kick I needed to sort myself out. I am now so much happier as a person and have learned so much about myself and our relationship. I honestly do not believe I could have made these changes if my husband hadn't left: it was such a life-changing jolt and moment of clarity.

However, he has barely spoken to me in the past six months and I have only seen him about once a month for a very short time (to pick up mail, etc.) I do not feel that he has ever talked about why he left, or why he wouldn't give me a chance to show him who I am now or talk about what went wrong in our relationship, or why he didn't stay and try to work on the relationship rather than just leave."

Change is difficult, especially when you're not getting any encouragement or feedback from your husband. Worse still, he could be cold, angry, or dismissive. At this point, it is very easy to become disheartened and forget the progress that you've made. So let's recap what you've achieved and how it has changed the situation. Firstly, you have apologized for past mistakes. Secondly, you have recognized which strategies you thought were helping save your marriage but were pushing him farther away, and stopped them. Thirdly, you have started to listen—really listen—and have a better idea what needs to change in the long term for your relationship to thrive. Finally, you are ready for the next phase of your fight back: implementing change.

The well-made plan

It is fine to have an overall goal, such as saving your marriage. However, when faced by hostility or, perhaps even worse, apathy, it is easy to be blown off course, start to despair, and give up hope. In contrast, if you have a detailed plan with lots of smaller goals, you are less likely to lose your way or be discouraged. So how can you test whether you have a well-made plan? Ask yourself if it is SMART:

Specific

Measurable

Achievable

Realistic

Timed (that is, with a date for completion)

For example, a Specific goal might be to have sex twice a week. It is also Measurable because you can look back at the end of the week or month and check how often you've been intimate. If your husband is angry or withdrawn and refuses to engage, it might not be Achievable. If you secretly expect one small change to achieve a breakthrough, your plan is not particularly Realistic—although as part of a larger portfolio of changes, it might make a significant contribution. Finally, if your mother-in-law is about to come and stay or your husband has to work late to complete end-of-year reports, it is not well-Timed.

Finding structure and focus

Most women lose hope because they are rushing around in circles—trying everything and anything to make things better—rather than being focused on SMART changes. So here are five key questions to ask yourself:

What is my goal? I would like you to have around three intermediate goals to support your main goal, of saving your marriage, or getting your husband to fall back in love. They could be something about improving communication, such as becoming a better listener, or something personal, such as being less of a perfectionist. They could be something practical like greeting him when he comes home or buying some suspenders and silk stockings. They could be something fun for both of you, for instance going away for a romantic weekend, or something for the whole family, like a day out at a fairground. If you are uncertain about what your husband might appreciate, think back to what he has always complained about but, in the past, you have discounted or ignored.

What are my resources? By this I mean, what personal qualities will help you to reach this goal. It could be, for example, your love for your husband, the support of your mother (she will babysit) or this book. It might be personal insight, determination ("I never give up without a fight") or twenty years of marriage. At times like this, it is easy to overlook just how much you have going for yourself.

What are my obstacles? This question is aimed at predicting possible problems. Obstacles might be personal, for example, "I tend to overanalyze and end up depressing myself," or "I don't like my body." They may also concern your circumstances: "Our son has special needs," or "I'm worried about the health of my father."

What changes do I need to make? Think about your obstacles and what you might need to do to overcome them. For example: "Whenever I start thinking about 'our problem,' I'll set an alarm on my cell phone to go off in ten minutes and tell myself that is enough for now," or "I'll give up looking at magazines and websites that pore over the imperfections in famous women's bodies." Try to come up with changes that are SMART.

What would support these changes? This is about making small changes that will help to turn your intermediate goals into a reality. For example, "I will take a yoga class to help me unwind, destress, and improve my general fitness."

For each of your intermediate goals, go through all the questions and write down a few key prompts, to provide structure and focus for the week ahead. For example, "I am going to listen to my husband more and let him finish what he's saying without interrupting. If I feel tempted, I will count to twenty." From time to time, go back and refresh your intermediate goals.

What if it is still not enough?

You wouldn't be human if you didn't sometimes feel overwhelmed by negative thoughts or feel down and depressed. You're doing your very best and either your husband doesn't really notice or he still can't commit ...

"My boyfriend still insists he can't give our relationship another try, even though we've made progress bringing the underlying causes into the open. He says he 'can't rule out the possibility' of giving it another go sometime in the future, but for now he wants to be alone and deal with his feelings on his own. How can I show him things have changed, if we don't have the opportunity to try at our relationship—even less so if he moves out and we have no contact? The relationship was blissfully happy until we stopped communicating and the arguments started ... Please help!"

Fortunately, these sorts of doubts and anxieties can be useful, because once problems are at the surface they can at least be discussed. However, when you're faced with a set back or a block, it is hard to approach them in a constructive manner and easy to let them undermine you. So what's the difference?

Five worst things to do if you're losing faith

Coming back from "I don't love you anymore" is a long and arduous journey, so perhaps it's not surprising that you might be tempted by a few coping strategies that might take the edge off your pain, but actually make things worse.

Push for an answer

When you're going through a tough time, one of the main ways of coping is to look for light at the end of the tunnel. No wonder you're seeking reassurance that your husband will "keep an open mind" or keep trying to make him agree that "staying together is the preferred goal." At your lowest moments, you would rather have a decision, even if it's not the outcome you want, rather than bear the uncertainty anymore.

Why this doesn't work: The only answer that he can give, at the moment, is that he is unhappy, doesn't know what he wants, or that you should call it a day. It might give you a burst of relief when you know the answer, but five minutes later you will be begging him to think again. On the other hand, uncertainty is your friend. It buys you time to work on your relationship.

Self-medicate

When I'm helping men through this program, I spend a lot of time stopping them from dampening down their feelings with alcohol, pornography, or attention from other women (even when they're trying to save their marriage). Fortunately, women are less likely to self-medicate in such obviously destructive ways, but they do take the edge off their panic with comfort foods or bouts of "retail therapy."

Why this doesn't work: If money is an issue between you and your husband, running up bills is going to make everything worse. Instead of concentrating on improving communication, you will be arguing over whether your daughter really needs that new top. If you have a tendency to reach for junk foods, you'll experience a low after the sugar rush has passed and end up feeling worse, as well as possibly triggering another round of destructive coping mechanisms.

Vent your feelings

You have all these painful feelings inside and if only you can get them out you'll feel better; even if it won't change anything, it will help you cope. In the same vein, telling him some home truths will get everything off your chest, make you feel lighter and perhaps shock him into taking a proper look at his behavior.

Why this doesn't work: I'm sure you've read enough of this book to know that this is not going to help. You'll either make him feel that your marriage is beyond help or that he can't trust the "reasonable" and "assertive" you, because, any moment now, the Dr. Jekyll mask is going to slip and he'll be faced with Mr. Hyde again. However, there is some sense behind this strategy, because you do need to offload. However, I would ask you not to do it to your husband. Write everything down on a piece of paper or put it in your private diary. In this way, you can step back and take a long, calm look at your feelings.

Let other people talk you down

You're feeling miserable so it seems sensible to offload to friends, family, and anybody else who will listen. Because these people love you, they want you to feel better. Unfortunately, they are often uncomfortable with the extremes of despair that accompany coping with your husband falling out of love. So it is no surprise that they suggest accepting the inevitable or throwing in the towel. Alternatively, your friends will question your judgment: "I wouldn't have rolled over and let him walk all over me," or your sister-in-law will pass on some piece of family insight, such as his mother thinking you're not a good wife, that will floor you and give you sleepless nights.

Why this doesn't work: Your friends and family can't see the bigger picture, especially when they are confronted by your pain, and they are not sure what you want from them. Next time you need to offload, explain that you're looking for a chance to talk, some sympathy, and lots of support, but there is no need to give advice. Ultimately, you know what is best for you.

Ignore the problems

If your husband is cold or snappy, it is tempting to walk away and wait until he is in a better mood. Similarly, when the atmosphere in the house drops below freezing point, you walk on eggshells, or busy yourself with work or the children. Alternatively, you will give yourself a pep talk and rationalize away your fears.

Why this doesn't work: If you're feeling depressed or anxious, there could be a good reason. Perhaps you've been making some stupid mistakes and need to up your game. Perhaps your husband is being negative because you've made a wrong diagnosis of the underlying problems, or you're heading in the right direction but pushing too far, too fast. Whatever the situation, treat your feelings as your allies: listen to them and hear what they have to tell you. In this way, something that seems destructive—his negative feelings—may be turned into something constructive.

Five helpful things to do when you're losing faith

Even if you're making all the right moves—listening to your husband, acknowledging his feelings, and making SMART changes—there will be times when you're tired, stressed, and feeling down. So here are five ways of keeping sane when the going gets tough.

Cut yourself some slack

Change is difficult and it takes time to replace unhelpful habits with helpful ones. I never worry about setbacks, unless people don't learn anything from them. Accept you will feel down or that your husband is angry or hopeless; this is much better than either one or both of you suppressing your feelings, because that's what got you into this trouble in the first place.

Why this works: Instead of running yourself down, and getting depressed and demotivated, you can look back over what went wrong and fine-tune your plan. So be kind to yourself; you are going through one of the biggest challenges life can throw at you and you're doing OK.

Live in the moment

Instead of worrying about past mistakes or being anxious about the future, focus on making it through today and the next seven days. What are the possible pitfalls over the weekend? When are you likely to feel down? What could head off those problems? If you find yourself thinking farther into the future, bring your focus back to today and tomorrow.

Why this works: Although we spend a lot of time thinking about the past or planning the future, we can live only in the present. So whenever you find yourself worrying about some distant tomorrow, tell yourself: "This is the age of uncertainty. I can't change the past and I can't know the future, but I can make today better."

Put yourself in your husband's shoes

When you're upset, it is easy to focus on *what* your husband has done rather than *why*. So instead of listing all the hurtful things, step back and try to understand what is driving his behavior. Time and time again, people behave badly because they are frightened. So ask yourself why your husband is so fearful? You most probably know the answer already. He is frightened of letting down his defenses and getting hurt again. He is frightened that he might stay, but find himself in the same place five years down the line. He is frightened that things between you will never change.

Why this works: Imagine that your husband is holed up in a deep, dark cave. Instead of trying to blast or starve him out, I'd like you to light a fire and start roasting something delicious. Putting yourself into his shoes will help you to understand, be kind, and compassionate and this, in turn, will encourage him to put aside his fears and come out into the light.

Go to a good place

If your thinking has tipped over from helpful reflection into obsessing, a good strategy is to imagine yourself in a good place. This can be somewhere that you have always enjoyed or felt safe—perhaps a vacation home from your childhood or sitting on your grandmother's lap—or somewhere in your imagination, such as a deserted beach with crickets singing in the dunes. Alternatively, it could be an activity that is engrossing and calming, for example going for a run, doing a crossword or baking.

Why this works: While self-medicating tries to block out feelings, going to a good place is a temporary distraction. Where self-medicating turns off your brain, going to a good place allows it to keep working in the background. Often when you're engrossed in something all-consuming and least expecting it, an answer or a useful insight will pop into your mind.

Read this book again

Instead of relying on your friends and supporters for advice, the answer might be in this book (or another of my books or one by another author). Reading is a good way of getting a new insight.

Why this works: Good books have many ideas and countless pieces of wisdom. It is not so much that you can't absorb everything at the first sitting, but that different things will strike you at different places on your journey. This is especially important if you tend to wolf down self-help books for the comfort and hope that they offer. Although you may take away the main message—for example, you can win back your husband—it is only when you return and read slowly that you can start to learn and grow.

"I never really loved you"

Sometimes it is hard to keep faith, because the message from your husband is so overwhelmingly negative that it makes you lose all hope:

> *"My husband says he's been feeling a disconnect from the beginning of our marriage, but couldn't say it for fear of hurting me. But he doesn't want to cause further damage and now wants a life that he wants to live. I cannot express in words how hard it has been to hear 'I don't feel anything for you' from a man I have loved wholeheartedly for so many years. He is my first love and, in all our years together, he has many times said no one can love me more than he does! Just before he went on his last business trip he expressed his love, so it was impossible to believe my ears."*

Whatever way your husband words the message "I never really loved you," it is a horrible thing to hear. It seems to attack the very foundations of your marriage. However, there is one good thing about the declaration: it is out in the open. Once something like this has been said, rather than floating around in his head, it can be tested in the real world. Sometimes, he will probably realize "I never loved you" is an exaggeration. He did feel something when he walked down the aisle, just not the dramatic "can't sleep, can't eat, can't think of anything but you" drama of the movies. Sometimes, men realize that they were depressed when they confessed and that made them exaggerate their feelings. Sometimes, they will realize what counts is right now—how you feel about each other today—rather than what happened ten or twenty years ago.

So how do you help your husband to progress from the bleakness of "I never really loved you" to something more nuanced and less desperate. I know you will want to debate what love is or tell him that life isn't like the movies. However it will be much better to listen, to ask questions to draw him out, and to really understand. Otherwise, you are on one side saying, "There are more important things than romantic love,"—which might be true—but he is on the other side thinking, "She's not taking me seriously, she's not interested in my feelings and we have different goals in life." By all means, tell him what love means to you, but respect his position and don't try to convince him that he is wrong.

Next, try to draw out what he means by "connected" or "truly in love." He could be talking about your sex life being predictable or disappointing. In which case, it is important to consider if he has a point or not (however harshly put). If your sex life could be improved and this has been a regret for you too, explain how you've been feeling and commit to tackling the underlying problems. Don't accuse him of having an affair or "feelings" for another woman—if you think this is the case, I'll address the issue in Part Two—as he will either get defensive or go on the attack. Your job at this stage is to find out as much as possible about his take on love. It is quite likely that this goes back a long way, maybe even to his childhood.

Finally, and this is the hardest part, don't take it so personally. I know, it is personal. Of course, you could have expressed your feelings more or been less wrapped up in the kids or your job (but you're going to do something about that). However, he has to take responsibility too for holding his emotional cards close to his chest, whether it was because he was frightened of getting hurt, did not expect love (because he received only qualified love as a child), or did not trust his own feelings (and let the green shoots of love grow into the jungle of emotions described in romantic books, songs, and movies). If you can stop taking these comments personally and think about them as much about his failings as your own, you will be less defensive, less likely to panic, and more able to listen.

"It's too late" and "I can't change my feelings"

There is no ending to the depressing and seemingly hopeless statements made by people who have fallen out of love.

"My husband and I managed to rebuild our lives after he had a major crisis with his feelings for me three years ago. However, he has continued to work too hard to the detriment of our family life. Last week, when he was due home, he never came and just sent a short text message hinting of his inability to cope any more with me and the situation. I honestly was not aware of a situation. I simply felt frustrated and disappointed that we shared so little time together and he always seemed to be working too hard. I am crushed that he never talked to me about his feelings. I have tried to communicate more, as this has always been a problem, but he keeps it all in. He is adamant he won't have marriage counseling. He seems content with his change of feelings and believes that work can sustain him and that he doesn't need us anymore. I want to fight for us, but he is shutting me out."

Since your husband has told you that he doesn't love you anymore, you've probably had hundreds of conversations trying to make sense of the situation and find a way forward. It can be particularly frustrating if you keep hitting "I can't change my feelings." It seems like a complete dead end because if his feelings don't change, he won't fall in love again and who wants to be in a loveless marriage?

However, feelings are not independent things that float around in the heart, they are based on events and thoughts. So while I never challenge my clients feelings, because they know when they feel sad, angry, or in love, I will challenge thoughts and how someone interprets an event. For example, you send your husband a chatty text. If he does not reply, you think, "He can't even be bothered to reply to a simple text. He can't love me." With this interpretation, your feelings will probably turn to despair. If you think, "Perhaps his battery has run down," or "He's really busy at work," then your feelings will be disappointment. So how can you use this knowledge to combat the belief "I can't change my feelings?"

If you start to communicate better, there is less chance for your husband to interpret your behavior as unloving or controlling and his feelings will begin to soften. If you provide more positive events—rather than getting angry and adding more negative ones—for his list, the balance will begin to tip and he will view your relationship more positively. Finally, his feelings will start to become more loving.

What about: "It's too late" and "I don't know what I want?" These statements are only a problem if you are pressing for a decision at this precise moment. If, instead, you remember that this is the age of uncertainty and put off talking about the future, you can focus on improving your relationship today and let tomorrow take care of itself.

Whatever negatives your husband comes out with, try to thank him. After all, you have made a significant step forward. Your communication has improved. You have a better understanding of your relationship and of how to resolve the problems. And most importantly, once you understand your husband's thought processes, you can make a better case for staying together. So openness and honesty—however tough to hear—is better than him clamming up and walking away.

Finally, if you have managed to listen calmly without becoming overwhelmed with anger or tears or begging for another chance (and making him feel guilty), I want you to give your-self a pat on the back. It is important to remember that you are going through a huge test at the moment and every time you are able to report your feelings (rather than act them out) and listen rather than argue, you are putting down the foundations for better communication—and that's the key to saving your relationship.

The importance of "framing" your story

When it comes to who wins an argument, it is seldom the person with the best grasp of the facts or the best debater, but the one with the most convincing story. So how do you frame your current situation, so that it is not dominated by your husband's negative message ("I don't love you anymore") and allow your positive one ("We can turn this around") to be heard?

This idea comes from Professor Marshall Ganz, who dropped out of Harvard to organize migrant workers in the sixties, but returned thirty years later to finish his degree and teach a new generation what he'd learned about motivating people and achieving changes. At the core of his philosophy is the idea that you need to make your pitch in three parts:

Why you feel called to act (Story of Self)
How this relates to the audience (Story of Us)
Challenge this action seeks (Story of Now)

The best example comes from Barack Obama's speech to the 2004 Democratic Convention. At this point, he was just a little-known candidate for the US Senate. His speech not only electrified the audience but put him on the map, and paved the way for his becoming President just four years later. His story was incredibly simple.

I am the son of a Kenyan goatherder running for Senate (Self).
A symbol of American meritocracy (Us).
Threatened by the elitist policies and cronyism of the Bush White House (Now).

Of course, this story played well because Obama had "framed" it in a way guaranteed to resonate with his audience. The American Dream is built on the idea that anybody can rise to the top and Obama had cast himself as a living example: someone with no special privileges and from Hawaii, one of the smallest and most out-of-the-way states. (A sharp contrast with George W. Bush, whose father had been President and had every advantage money could buy.) His audience were ordinary men and women who were also struggling to get ahead and could readily identify with his ambitions. However, here is the clever part. By supporting Obama, they were effectively cheering themselves on. Obama's success proved that the American Dream worked and, by extension, that they too could climb to the top; he was promising to take away the blocks that were holding them back, thereby doubling their chances. So how does this relate to your situation?

Your husband is currently framing the story in this way:

I've fallen out of love (Story of Self).
Our marriage is fatally flawed (Story of Us).
It would be better for everyone if we split up (Story of Now).

Of course, there are variations on the themes. For "Us," it might be, "we are wrong for each other," "we've tried before and nothing really changes," or "I don't think we can work this out." For "Now," it might be "I want to find someone else before I'm too old" or "I'm exhausted by all the arguing and fights and can't carry on any longer."

Maybe your husband is framing the story in a different way, but before you can start to combat it, you need to be clear what you're up against. So write down your husband's story to himself, you and the world. This should be reasonably easy as you've probably heard it a million times before.

Story of Self:
Story of Us:
Story of Now:

Next, write down your own story. Don't try to dress it up, just give the core of your message:

Story of Self:
Story of Us:
Story of Now:

Why your story is falling on deaf ears

Most wives will put down, "I still love you" (or some variation on the theme) for "Self." I think there is a more convincing story, but we'll come to that later. However, I have heard some really weak stories. For example: "The children are in the middle of their exams"—which reinforces the idea that you just want him as a father and he'll tell himself that he can still be a father in an apartment down the road; other weak examples are: "I've been struggling with depression," which sounds helpless, or "It's not fair, after everything I've done for you," which sounds bitter and accusatory. I've also heard some uninspiring stories of "Us." For example: "Don't expect marriage to be a bed of roses," "You won't do any better," or "That woman is just using you."

If you're having trouble framing your story, think of it as a banner to march behind and something to put fire in your belly to keep going through the tough times. Therefore your story must be positive and aspirational:

Story of Self: *I've had a huge wake-up call.*
Story of Us: *I have to thank you for stopping me from drifting.*
Story of Now: *With your bravery (of owning up to the problem), all my determination (and the changes I'm making), this is the chance to have a truly fulfilling relationship.*

Obviously, this is just an example. To be truly powerful, your story must be something that speaks to your situation, your strengths, and your goals. So take your time to think it through.

Love Coach's Three Key Things to Remember

- This is the age of uncertainty. Use the time to implement change, prove that you are listening, and that you accept your husband's feelings, because this will make him believe that things can truly change.

- If there are setbacks, you need to acknowledge and learn from them, rather than panic or give up hope.

- Instead of trying to knock down your husband's negative story, take the initiative by framing the situation in a positive way.

CHAPTER SIX

Why am I still stuck?

"I have been with my fiancé for eight years and engaged for one year. Five months ago, he dropped the bombshell that his feelings had changed and that he no longer saw a future together. He told me this on the day his dad had major surgery to remove a brain tumor. With a history of depression before we met, I was convinced those were the real reasons he was unhappy and that it was nothing to do with our relationship.

I was in shock for the first few months after the bombshell and didn't quite know what to do, so I just tried to carry on and be there for him. I encouraged him to go to his doctor and he was given antidepressants, and I hoped that they would help to clear things up in a couple of months. We had a few talks periodically, which all ended with me becoming emotional and getting very upset. I wanted answers and he wasn't able to give me any. He couldn't tell me when his feelings changed or why or how they had changed.

When he invited me to his mom's birthday meal in October, I thought things were getting better, but a few days later we had another talk which ended with us breaking up. It just felt as if he had given up without trying everything possible, that the relationship I felt was so special wasn't worth saving in his eyes. He told me that it was too late, that our relationship had gone past the point of saving, but he didn't want to fall out with me and he did miss me. We left that last face-to-face meeting with a hug and with me saying that I didn't think it was ever too late, that we should try to be friends; and he suggested we meet up again. I know I have to work on making myself happy first, but is it ever really too late?"

You're not only doing all the work to save your marriage, but you're getting little or no positive feedback from your husband.

Worse still, he is distant, downright dismissive, or even hostile. Nevertheless, you have kept the faith for months on end and framed your story in a positive way, rather than begging or getting angry. Despite all your efforts, you are still no further forward. In the final chapter of this section, I'm going to explore some of the reasons for the roadblock and suggest some ways around it.

My husband has become a stranger

One of the stories we tell ourselves about love and relationships is that when we're young it's OK to experiment, sow our wild oats and make a few mistakes. In that way, we will have learnt who we are and be ready to settle down. So far so good, but it comes with an unspoken assumption. Once we are married, we will remain that same person, with the same needs from now until forever. Of course, we'll have a few more wrinkles, but we will remain fundamentally unchanged. The message is reinforced in popular songs such as "Stay as sweet as you are" or we're told not to change because Billy Joel loves us "Just the way you are." It's part of the soul mate myth: of finding someone with whom we will click on such a profound level that all problems and differences fall away and we live happily ever after.

However, life and growing older changes us. In an ideal world, we would discuss our unhappiness and negotiate with our partner about what needs to change. In this way, we can evolve and find different priorities in our thirties, forties, fifties, sixties and beyond. Unfortunately, lots of people are frightened that their partner will be unhappy with change. After all, it's not what they signed up for and probably they're quite happy with the old deal, thank you. So the person who wants, or needs, to change swallows their unhappiness, and soldiers on and on and on. Until, one day, they explode with unhappiness—and becomes domineering and demand change, rather than being assertive and negotiating it. No wonder their partners think they are strangers.

These problems are exacerbated if you were childhood sweethearts and have been "together forever." It is natural, from time to time, to look back at the paths you didn't take. What if I'd gone off to university? What if I'd followed my ambitions to be a rock star? What if we hadn't had children so young? What if I'd seen a bit more of the world before I settled down? It's part of growing older and everybody goes through it. However, it is more acute for childhood sweethearts who have had less opportunity to experiment. Around the midpoint of our lives, we become more aware of our mortality—perhaps one of our parents dies— and we start to calculate how much time we've got left and what we want to do with it. During this soul searching, everything is up for debate and that includes our relationships, especially in two particular scenarios.

Firstly, your husband finds your marriage disappointing because he hasn't felt special or cherished for several years. If he falls into this category, I hope my book has already given you some strategies for combating the problem. Secondly, the two of you have been so close and done so much together that it is hard for him to work out where being a husband and father ends and being a person in his own right begins. He will ask himself, "Who am I?" and "What do I want from life?" As I hope you're beginning to realize, these are very difficult questions to answer and many people shy away from them. We want simple and easy solutions. So, many men go to the gym, to change the way they look, or go out with their work colleagues for a drink, to have a bit of fun.

Alternatively, some men (and women too around forty) are frightened of looking too deeply for fear of what they might find and the impact on the family. What if they do a lot of soul-searching and discover that they are deeply unhappy, can't be themselves, or that their wives are stopping them from achieving their goals? Unfortunately, suppressing these thoughts doesn't make them go away, but instead makes them multiply until the husband confesses, "I don't love you anymore" and "You're holding me back." For many wives, this is a complete shock. They haven't prevented their husband from doing anything. In fact, they have positively encouraged him in all his endeavors and been happy for him to let his hair down with the boys.

So if your husband has become a stranger or seems to be going through some sort of midlife crisis, what should you do?

Embrace change

We don't like change. It is uncomfortable and scary and we do our best to avoid it. "What if we grow apart?" "What if he changes and wants different things?" "What if I can't be the sort of woman who likes camping?" It is easy to catastrophize and imagine that it is the end of your relationship.

However, while you are panicking, it is easy to overlook the upside. It would be a dull world if we were exactly same at seventeen and forty-seven. It might feel comfortable to know someone inside out or be able to predict the way they will react, but it is also incredibly boring. What's more, "possessing" someone kills passion; after all, we desire what we haven't got or, at least, don't feel 100 percent sure of. I bet that since your husband has threatened to leave, your interest in him has sky-rocketed!

It is good, from time to time, to audit your life and put everything up for discussion. The problem is when some subjects are off-limits, like your relationship. As I've explained before, negative thoughts are better out than in, so they can be tested in the real world. Anything that is suppressed and "unmentionable" grows powerful and becomes even scarier in the shadows.

So thank your husband for being honest and explain how his soul-searching has encouraged you to do something similar; then tell him what you would like to change.

Be honest with yourself

Imagine everything your husband says is true—at least from his perspective; have you truly supported his changes? Have you talked down his plans for starting a business, because you were worried about losing a steady income or taking on a large debt? Although you haven't stopped him from going out, have you used subtler ways of getting your way, for example, sighing or sniping ("out again"), or shown your displeasure by pushing him away when he's made overtures for sex? Perhaps you've just assumed, "We like a nice family weekend," and not checked whether your husband would rather, for example, be climbing mountains or competing in yacht races. If any of these thoughts strike a chord, make a fulsome apology.

110

Become part of the change

If you genuinely believe that you have supported your husband, try going the extra mile. If he's always wanted a motorbike, go along with him to the showrooms and look over the models. Understand the difference between a city and a touring bike, so that you can help him weigh up the pros and cons. Could you become involved in this activity? Even if it is only occasionally, in good weather and for the most interesting destinations, like Route 66. Ultimately, does it matter, for example, if he joins a group of other middle-aged men and reclaims his youth by playing rock music in local bars? Doesn't he deserve a more sporty car after years of driving a family one? Think about how you can help with his project, rather than just point out problems, and become an ally instead of the enemy.

Follow my program

Although "I don't know what I want but I don't want you" feels deeply personal, don't let your panic stop you from working on your communication skills, becoming more assertive, and a better listener. Your husband is saying, "I don't want my old life," and that's fine, because circumstances change (children grow up and don't need us so much) and life changes us. He is not necessarily saying "I don't want you," rather "I don't want the same old you." And again, that's fine, because you can change and grow too.

Six common causes of emotionally absent men

If you've looked at your own contribution to your husband's existential crisis, made a fulsome apology for what you regret, worked on being assertive, and tried to become part of his support team, but he still seems emotionally absent, there could be more going on than meets the eye.

> "My husband has left me after 18 years (15 married) and one week later has a new girlfriend. I think the trigger was our business going into administration. He had built it up over seven years to a multimillion-dollar turnover and it was almost like our

third child. When the business went under, he found another job 200 miles away, moved there, and concentrated on his new job. He was extremely fortunate that he found a well-paid job so quickly. There were considerable financial ramifications to the business going into administration, so it was a real relief. So four months later, our daughters and I moved, rented a property, and relocated. I found it hard to settle in, having left my support network of ten years behind, but after five months or so, I was beginning to feel better about it all.

We didn't have much spare money, so going out together wasn't really an option, with no family particularly nearby. Anyway, by November last year, I had begun to notice a change in my husband. He was distracted and withdrawn. I asked him about it and he just said he felt numb, had trouble sleeping, and almost didn't want to be happy. I immediately thought he might be depressed, but he refused to go to the doctors. He distanced himself from the girls and me, although we still cuddled up in bed. Then, one day, he came home from work and I could tell instantly something was wrong. His demeanor was different and he told me, 'I don't deserve you; you deserve someone better; I can't love you like you want to be loved' and so on.

Four days later he admitted there was a colleague at work he had feelings for and he moved out. They started dating and slept together. Meanwhile, I tried to hold things together for our daughters, who initially knew nothing. A couple of weeks later, he told them he didn't want to be married to me anymore."

As this letter illustrates, there is often a series of overlapping problems that could have brought your husband to this point. It is important to be aware of the full range, rather than focus on the most painful—the other woman; otherwise, you risk investing her with more power than she really has and not diagnosing the real cause of the crisis. So what are the most common causes of men becoming emotionally absent?

General stress

It could be the drip, drip, drip of money worries, long commutes, or the demands of a disabled child, but all the joy seems to have drained out of his life. This cause seldom explains why the crisis has happened right now or why you might be stuck, but adds to the general background of unhappiness.

What to do: It is important to have some fun in your relationship and small treats to look forward to. It does not have to be expensive, perhaps a takeout and a DVD, but have something enjoyable to share together.

Death of a parent

There is nothing that reminds us more powerfully that our time on earth is limited than the death of a loved one. If it is our parents, we think "It will be me next," and "How am I going to make the rest of my life meaningful?" If your parents were judgmental or dictatorial, there can be a sense of freedom mixed in with the grief: "I can do what I want rather than what I should do."

What to do: Men are brought up to be emotionally self-sufficient. Instead of talking about the complex feelings associated with grief, they focus on the practical stuff: organizing the funeral, winding up the estate, and so on. Your husband will probably tell you that he's fine or push you away, but don't be fooled by the surface. It takes normally two years to recover. So look for opportunities that occur naturally, like someone coming to collect his father's stamp collection, to reflect on his loss, and let him open up in his own good time.

Business failure

There is nothing more important to a man than providing for his family and being a success. So his business folding, losing his job, or being passed over for promotion are not just setbacks, but attacks on his identity and even his masculinity. I don't think women truly understand the body blow it can be, because they tend to spread their sources of well-being and identity, by for example being a good mother, daughter, friend, and so on. There might be a whole host of rational reasons for a career crisis—the global downturn, companies outsourcing jobs abroad, or government cuts—but to your husband, it will seem like a personal failure.

What to do: Instead of general praise, such as "you're a great dad," which can seem empty, try using Descriptive Praise. As explained in Chapter Four (see page 83), this focuses on something specific. For example: "I admire how you've approached looking for a job as if it is a job." Even if he is slumped on the couch and doing very little, praise the steps toward recovering his sense of purpose, for example "It was really helpful to come home to a home-cooked meal," rather than complaining about what he hasn't done ("At the very least, you could have pushed a vacuum cleaner around the place.") You need to convey the message that you believe in him through both your words and actions.

Alcohol issues

When someone is unhappy and feels that there is no way out of their problems, they look for ways to cope. While women off-load onto their friends, many men keep their cares to themselves—either because that's what their father did, they don't want to burden their partners or they can't even admit how bad it's got. One of the easiest, most available, and socially acceptable ways for men to switch off is having a drink. Unfortunately, it is easy to tip over from using alcohol to unwind, into abusing it and into addiction problems. While in our twenties and thirties, heavy drinking can be managed because the body recovers more quickly, many men in their forties start to have a real problem—including passing out, memory loss, violence, and poor decision-making. No wonder you feel you can't reach him if his emotions are being anesthetized with alcohol—or some other form of addictive behavior, like gambling, cocaine, or smoking marijuana.

What to do: You have probably tried talking to him, but he's minimized the problems or got angry and defensive. Hopefully, his admission about falling out of love has made you look at your relationship through new eyes and what seemed unpleasant but fairly tolerable behavior before is now unacceptable. If he won't seek advice, please get help for yourself from one of the services that supports the families of addicts such as Al-Anon.

Depression

I would be very surprised if your husband is not depressed. As I explained in Chapter One, most men outsource their emotional welfare to their wives (and most women are happy to accept the task). Unfortunately, for whatever reasons, you have been preoccupied, angry, or overwhelmed with your own stuff and have not been able to sort him out. Perhaps he is such a people-pleaser that he has either never articulated his needs, or does not truly know what they are, but expected you to second-guess; maybe he hoped that if he made everybody else happy they would reciprocate. Whatever the reasons, his life is no longer working.

In this situation, we naturally withdraw, close in ourselves, and reflect. In effect, our emotions are telling us that something is wrong and we need to attend to it. However, most men don't listen to their feelings, but blank them out with alcohol or tell themselves to man up and get on with it. So instead of using the natural response of being depressed to learn about themselves and adapt their lives, they carry on regardless, drink more, or work harder to distract themselves. To use a metaphor that will resonate with men, it is like the oil light coming on in the car dashboard and, instead of topping off the engine, driving on and on and on. Eventually, the engine will grind to a halt. This is exactly what happens if you don't listen to the clues; your body will shut down and force you to listen. You start suffering from depression and have difficulty getting out of bed in the morning or find the motivation for anything. If you still don't listen, you will tip over into clinical depression or a mental breakdown.

What to do: Ultimately, he needs to take responsibility for his own life rather than outsourcing it to other people—and then attacking them for not doing a good job. I know this sounds an incredibly hard mountain to climb. However, if you've been following my program and become assertive yourself, rather than domineering or passive, it will encourage him to be assertive back and ask for what he needs.

Of course, it is worth encouraging him to consult his doctor as medication may help. There is a form of counseling that is particularly effective for depression called Cognitive Behavioral Therapy (CBT). It is also more popular with men than general counseling as it tends to be shorter—about six sessions—and focuses on learning skills rather than just talking. Some doctors will prescribe a course. As I explained earlier, it is important not to pressurize your husband or see pills or therapy as a magic cure. If he won't seek help, you have to respect his wishes rather than sulk, make a sarcastic comment, or get angry. Instead ask him, "What do you intend to do instead?" He will probably say something along the lines of that he'll wait and see or try to think positively. Follow up by enquiring about how you can help and agree to give his strategy an agreed amount of time, for instance three months, and review it again. In the meantime, focus on implementing my strategy of working on yourself and improving general communication.

Finally, don't keep asking him how he is feeling today, because it could remind him of his problems on a relatively good day and, if he's really down, you will not be able to reach him.

Another woman

I wouldn't be surprised if you've been reacting "Yes, but …" as this chapter has progressed. Yes, I've made some good points, but I'm avoiding the screamingly obvious: "He doesn't love me because he's fallen for another woman and he doesn't listen because he wants to run away with her and live happily every after." So let me explain why I've left the most obvious cause to last. If someone is feeling a failure, is depressed, or blanking out his feelings with alcohol, it will need an extremely strong emotion to cut through the grayness and help him to feel "alive" again.

Of course, another woman finding him attractive and interesting will boost his self-esteem, which is probably at an all-time low, but what is really dangerous is something I call "limerence." This is the crazy, walking-on-air part of falling in love and normally lasts somewhere between six months, when it is not reciprocated by the other person, and around eighteen months, when both parties have feelings for each other. Scientists have tracked the chemicals in the brain that bond us to other people and found that they are at their peak over a similar amount of time.

(I explain more about limerence in *I Love You But I'm Not in Love with You*.)

What to do: It is important to understand how you got from walking down the aisle—full of joy and love—to this crisis—full of despair and worry. Although you have only become aware of the depth of the problems relatively recently, they have probably been brewing for quite some time. Lot of things that people do to protect their marriages, such as going along with what their partner wants, not arguing, and burying differences, can lead to "I love you, but I'm not in love with you," where couples are friends rather than lovers. If this problem is not addressed, one or both partners will become resentful or fall completely out of love and, at that point, they will start to notice other people or be easily tempted. Hopefully, you will have identified the problems before they reach this dangerous point and you can put down the book at the end of this section.

Alternatively, your husband's "feelings" for another woman or "friendship" is at the mild end, rather than infatuation, and will be reasonably easy to unhook. Perhaps he is completely smitten and thinks he has found true love and has packed his bags. Whatever the circumstances, I will cover how to fight back in Part Two. However, please try to keep calm and process your feelings, rather than act impulsively and risk making everything worse.

Don't panic!

Whatever your circumstances, please try not to panic. I know you want to solve the problems now, or at least by tomorrow. However, you will end up putting yourself under unbearable stress, destroying your already tattered self-esteem, and risk pushing ahead too quickly:

"I have been with my boyfriend for ten years and have lived with him for seven. He works and I am a housewife (we have no children). Three weeks ago he said that he didn't love me anymore, that he saw me as a friend but not a lover. He told me that he's

felt this way for a long time and, for him, our relationship is totally over. Since then I have moved into the spare bedroom and he says that he would like us to work on our friendship and live as roommates.

I bought your books and have been trying to follow the techniques you lay out. I listened intently to what my boyfriend said were the reasons for him feeling this way and I looked at what was my responsibility. I made a fulsome apology and worked out what I needed to change in myself to improve these things. I tried taking the pressure off and started going back to normal living, but my boyfriend told me that this was making him uncomfortable. Because this behavior involved me trying to initiate your ideas on regaining limerence and trying to be affectionate I would kiss him and if I saw a cake or chocolate bar he likes I'd buy it for him. These are things he used to do for me, so I thought this was his love language. However he says he doesn't want any of the 'couple stuff' with me anymore and that these actions are making him feel unhappy at home.

Am I trying to progress things too quickly? He also said that because I'm upset I'm pushing him away and making him realize that there definitely isn't any hope for us as a couple. I still get very upset and angry, but I try to deal with these emotions myself (I have started a diary as your books suggest) so as not to burden my boyfriend. It has only been a few weeks and I'm concerned that I'm expecting things to change too quickly, but if the changes I implement and the techniques I try only push him away, what do I do instead?"

Sometimes in the rush to encourage your husband to fall back in love, you can minimize his unhappiness, and not really listen to his anger, but "love bomb" him instead. This is better than criticizing, nagging, and ignoring, but can just as easily push him away.

So if you're feeling stuck, it could be that you're moving too quickly, not acknowledging his genuine distress, or working enough on your own unhelpful behavior. In my experience, it normally takes about three months to change your communication style and for your husband to not only notice, but also begin to believe in, the changes. Ultimately, you have the whole of your life in front of you. Does it matter if takes a few months to resolve things? Most people mess up their marriage by ignoring problems—sometimes for years on end; then when things come to a head they destroy it by wanting an answer or to know where they stand almost immediately. So why not try flipping this around and put some urgency into facing the problems, but take your time finding a way forward?

I want to finish Part One in the same way that I started: by offering reassurance. You can turn around your relationship and get back the loving feelings. There will be setbacks and times when it feels you're taking one step forward and two steps back. Don't beat yourself up, but instead learn from what went wrong, so you can avoid that pitfall next time around.

Remember this is the age of uncertainty, so don't push for reassurance, bring up "the future" or ask about his feelings. Please be patient and understanding and, most importantly, aim to increase the ratio of positive to negative moments between you and your husband: more smiles, compliments, acts of kindness, small presents, listening, understanding, and acknowledging feelings.

Love Coach's Three Key Things to Remember

- If your husband is reassessing his life or looking to change something, become part of his support team rather than the enemy.

- It is easy to focus on another woman as the cause of your problems, rather than understanding why your marriage might have become vulnerable.

- It takes time to turn around your relationship. Make certain that you are truly listening to his pain and anger, rather than just trying to "love bomb" him.

Love Coach's Eighteen Key Things to Remember from Part One

To help you when you are feeling down or wondering why your husband is not responding, I've gathered together the most important lessons from Part One to keep you focused, to channel your energy into the most productive activities, and, ultimately, to win him back.

- More relationships end because of a wife's panic than a husband's determination to leave.

- Listen to your husband; really listen to what he has to say.

- Think everything through before you act.

- Men consider women to be experts on relationships and often unconsciously subcontract their feelings to them and then get angry when they don't make them happy.

- Most relationships deteriorate because of a variety of interlocking reasons.

- There is no one single magic bullet that will solve this crisis. However, better communication will lay the foundations for a better marriage.

- By apologizing for your mistakes, you will show your husband that you understand his unhappiness and are committed to changing yourself and the relationship for the better.

- The center of your fight-back plan is to be assertive, rather than passive or domineering. So don't swallow your needs, wants, and opinions and don't expect your husband to do the same either.

- Even if your husband is not willing to cooperate in saving your marriage, it does not stop you from working on your half of the communication.

- If your husband thinks that you spend the majority of your time complaining, nagging, or getting angry, he will feel all the joy is being sucked out of your relationship.

- Every interaction with your husband—however small and even if you're separated—is a chance to try out the skills you're learning.

- Focus on creating a sustainable sex life which places lovemaking at the center of your relationship.

- This is the age of uncertainty. Use the time to implement change and to prove that you are listening and that you accept your husband's feelings—this will make him believe that things can truly change.

- If there are setbacks, you need to acknowledge and learn from them, rather than panic or give up hope.

- Instead of trying to knock down your husband's negative story, take the initiative by framing the situation in a positive way.

- If your husband is reassessing his life or looking to change something, become part of his support team rather than the enemy.

- It is easy to focus on another woman as the cause of your problems, rather than understanding why your marriage might have become vulnerable.

- It takes time to turn around your relationship. Make certain that you are truly listening to his pain and anger rather than just trying to "love bomb" him.

PART TWO

He's Texting Someone Else

CHAPTER SEVEN

Why now?

When I first started my training, almost thirty years ago, my supervisor would always ask after I described a couple's problems: "Why now?" It was a good question as most marriages deteriorate slowly over many years. Although it is useful to understand the whole journey, it is vital to address the reasons why, after years of arguing, poor sex, or being taken for granted, the couple had pitched up at my door.

When it comes to dealing with "I don't love you anymore," I always take a twin approach. I work on both improving communication (because that's normally behind the long-term difficulties) and sorting out the immediate crisis. So why has your husband told you now that he doesn't love you? It could be a variety of reasons—from the seemingly trivial to the obviously serious. Perhaps it is the buildup of small matters. For example, you still haven't worn the lingerie that he bought for your birthday, so he's decided that you don't like sex and he's facing a lifetime of being sex-starved. Maybe you told him that it's madness to waste money on his flying lessons when the children need new computers, acting lessons, and a foreign exchange trip to improve their language skills. Suddenly, he's realized that his needs come last and he's facing a lifetime of drudgery to make everybody else happy. Alternatively, it could be something much bigger—like a brush with death, turning forty or restructuring at work.

However, more times than not, the answer to "why now" is another woman.

"After telling me 'I love you, but …' about a year ago, my husband suggested we take it one day at a time and see where it takes us. We carried on as normal, going out with friends and so on, but the physical side to our relationship seemed to be less and

less. As time went on, he became like a stranger to me, just me, anyone else saw the same person. His resentment ground me down so much that I started counseling because I feel like failure. In the back of my mind, I always thought there was something not quite right.

I recently discovered, by means of his cell phone account, that he had been in regular contact with a close friend of mine. It was constant: morning, noon, and night. This is the friend that we had socialized with, her husband too; been on vacation with, even the last one; and I had confided so much with. Last month alone there were 1,707 texts just to her number, not to mention numerous calls.

I challenged him and he denied being in contact with her. He continued to blame me for the failure of our marriage. I didn't admit to seeing the bills straight away, but eventually I couldn't take it anymore and showed him what I had seen. He still denied it even though it was there in black and white. I can't believe how anyone could be so cruel and devious ..."

Six types of other women

Discovering your husband is "involved" with another woman is horrible—even if it is just a mild flirtation. Your heart is racing, it's hard to swallow, it feels like a bag of cement is lodged in your stomach, and your mind is working overtime. However, it is important to try to keep calm and work out the degree of threat that this woman poses. In effect, there are six categories of "involved" and each needs a tailor-made response.

The Spark

There is somebody at work, at the gym, or maybe even one of your friends whom he suddenly notices. She might not have given him any encouragement, or maybe she's a bit extrovert and flirty, but he's noticed something: "I do have feelings," if he's been depressed; "I am attractive to women," after feeling neglected; or "There's more to life than drudgery," when he's going through some crisis where he's had to keep his head down and work extra hard. Whatever the circumstances, the other woman has lit a spark and got him thinking and it's not good news for your marriage.

Unfortunately, it's really hard to uncover a Spark and she might not even be a direct threat. For example, she could be happily married and just taking pity on a work colleague who seems down; maybe a bit of banter helps pass the long hours or she's just someone who shares his passion for, for example, medieval history. Perhaps she is offering a listening ear and taking his rather one-sided account of your marriage at face value. In many cases, the first sense of a Spark is when your husband starts saying things that don't sound like him; that's because he's parroting someone else's opinions or advice.

What to do: It is really hard to get the right balance for approaching a Spark—especially as it is mostly in his head. On one hand, you don't want to ignore the problem, but on the other, if you go in all guns blazing you will come across as trying to police his thoughts and feelings. After all, what's wrong with chatting with someone at a party or noticing how attractive they are? When your husband said, "I don't love you anymore," you probably asked, "Is there someone else?" Of course, he would have said no—because technically there isn't. So I would follow up with some supplementary questions: "Why did you tell me this now?," "Have you been getting advice on our relationship from someone else?," and "Have you found someone else particularly attractive?" Tell him that you will not get angry or blow his answers out of all proportion, but it would help you to understand. If he does come up with something, ask any follow-up questions and then thank him for his honesty. In this way, you will have shown that you will listen to him calmly and take on board his opinions and feelings. If he still says no, but your gut instincts tell you there is a Spark (or maybe something more), I would just accept that you're probably right and press on with saving your marriage as I outlined in Part One. The alternative is fighting to prove your hunch, which could be impossible, and getting his back up and stopping you from creating an alliance to turn around your relationship.

The Online Connection

The internet has blurred the lines between reality and fantasy, and social media has blurred the lines of friendship, with Facebook and similar sites encouraging us to "friend" casual acquaintances, people from our past and work colleagues and give unparalleled access to the minutiae of our lives and the family photograph album. So your husband can tell himself his activities are just a bit of fun or that he has signed up to an internet dating site to "see what was out there." In effect, he has put his online activity into a watertight box and told himself that what happens online stays online and therefore has no impact on his real flesh-and-bones life.

Unfortunately, he is being incredibly naive. At some point, online flirting has to progress to chatting on the telephone or meeting up, otherwise it will wither and die. Even if it does stay online—because your husband is "talking" to someone halfway around the world—it is still incredibly dangerous. In some cases, online friendships get very deep very quickly. After all, you can't go to the movie theater or down the bar with buddies, so there is nothing to do but talk and trade secrets. Under these circumstances, it is easy to think that you have found your soul mate and are destined to be together—especially when you don't need to deal with humdrum, everyday reality. In addition, people often play fast and loose with the truth or use the "high" of someone's attention to cover up holes in their lives.

What to do: There are two scenarios with this kind of woman (or women). Firstly, you will be told that it's all "a bit of fun" or his way of "unwinding" or "coping with a stressful job." He might even try to distract you by claiming that it's better than "going out and getting drunk" or that "I'm nowhere near as bad as this guy at work who hires prostitutes." I know it's going to be hard, but don't get drawn into a debate about the rights and wrongs of his behavior. It will go nowhere productive. You will get angry or tearful, he will clam up or storm out or go on the attack—and criticize your spending habits, the state of the house or your mother. Not only will this conversation be painful and destructive, but it will solve nothing.

Instead take the root of the problem very seriously and ask questions: "What is so stressful about your job?," "How do you feel when you come home?" or "How do you feel on Monday morning when you return to work?" Hopefully, you will get a better picture of your husband's unhappiness or realize the full extent of the pressure he's under. Feed back to him what you've discovered—this will make him feel heard and receptive, rather than defensive and closed up.

Finally, summarize his behavior on the internet—try not to sound too judgmental—and ask how that is going to solve his real-life problems. With luck, at this point, he will be ready to discuss changes to your relationship, his work practices, or getting professional help and you will have begun to form an alliance to save the situation.

Alternatively, he could claim he still "needs" this woman or is determined to believe he has found a soul partner. I will discuss these scenarios a little later.

The Special Friend

It's great that men and women mix more freely and have friends of the opposite sex. We are also much more likely to work in teams today and develop close relationships with our colleagues. There are a lot of advantages: the opposite sex is not a foreign land and we treat each other as equals. However, there is a downside too. It is easy to cross the line and move from being friends into having feelings for each other—and these feelings are not just friendship, but something much darker. Often it is hard to know the exact point when you start betraying your partner. It's fine to send a text that is not about work. It's fine to have a drink after work to wind down. It's fine to talk about problems when you're fed up. However, we all instinctively know that 1,707 texts in a month (over fifty a day) is not just a friendship, more a part-time job! One drink can turn into supper and perhaps a nightclub too—but somehow the "friends" do not tell their partners that the rest of the team went home hours earlier. Before too long, the off-loading about work problems turns into a detailed analysis of the friends' marriages and into sharing intimate secrets. At this point, and probably for a long time beforehand, it has changed from a friendship into something inappropriate. Let's return to the letter that opened this chapter:

"... How stupid have I been? I had caught my husband and my friend texting before, but they both said nothing was going on and they would stop. I just knew there was something more to this.

She has now split from her husband, divorced a couple of months ago, and the story is that my husband and her have been out on a few occasions and have kissed—that's all. He said he couldn't take it any further while we were still under the same roof; he wouldn't do that to me. Our kids hate the situation and say they will never accept them as a couple as do hers.

The thing is, I still love him so much and would still take him back. Sad, I know. Don't get me wrong: I do blame him, what an ego boost ... but I blame my friend mostly. She always said she wanted what I had, and I believe she went in for the kill when he was feeling down and vulnerable after his brother's death. I can't imagine what she has told him, obviously stuff to her advantage—let's face it, she has had enough ammunition from all the times I have poured my heart out to her. I don't know what to do; I'm not finding it easy to switch off my emotions."

If your partner has a Special Friend, you will probably already know her name. Especially at the beginning of the "relationship," when it was still reasonably innocent, he will have mentioned her over and over again—and probably rung alarm bells in your head. This is because when someone is consumed by interest for someone else, they cannot stop themselves from talking about their Special Friend—how she said that and how she likes this television program. At some point, your partner will have stopped talking about his Special Friend and you will think it's cooled down, but actually that's the very moment when it's hotted up and the "friends" either consciously or unconsciously know they have crossed the line and start covering their tracks.

What to do: Special Friends are really dangerous and notoriously difficult to combat. If you go on the attack, your husband will

swear that they are "just friends" and accuse you of being controlling, emasculating, and paranoid. As you can imagine, arguing about definitions of friendship and what is acceptable is not
going to help save your marriage—but it is incredibly easy to fall
into this trap.

Instead I would accept his definition; if they truly are friends,
then the relationship is open to public scrutiny. If you have not
met this woman, why doesn't he invite you to meet her? Hopefully, this will be enough to get a more honest answer. But if not,
you can move the discussion on. If they are truly friends, he will
be happy to open up his text and email account to you. I'm not
suggesting that you read their communications—otherwise you
will end up debating whether it's all right to put an "x" at the
end of a text or not—but to reveal the meta-data. (This is what
government agencies have been accused of gathering on their
citizens.) Basically, it shows how many messages and at what
times and to whom. It also shows how much money was spent
on credit cards and when. This kind of data often speaks for
itself—50 texts a day! However, it is particularly powerful when
cross-referenced with the official story of what happened. For
example, your husband was supposed to be out with his mates
for a beer, but the credit card account shows a meal for two in a
restaurant.

With luck, when presented with the extent of their communication, he will sober up and face reality. (Lots of men deceive
themselves about the extent and breadth of the deception and
truly believe it started later, they spoke less often and they spent
less money.) At this point, you can finally have an honest discussion about what happens next. I'll discuss the boundary between
appropriate and inappropriate friendship in the next chapter.

The Emotional Affair

If an inappropriate friendship isn't checked, it soon turns into an
emotional affair. At this point, your husband and the other
woman will have declared their feelings for each other. They
might have tried to stop, but their resolve soon weakens and they
are back to sharing texts and putting more and more energy into
their affair—and leaving their marriages with just the scraps. An

emotional affair does not include sex and the lovers will swear that they have "only kissed." At first sight, this doesn't sound so bad but, believe me, it's not the chaste kiss that you'd give your grandmother! These kisses are long and passionate—teenagers call this necking and sex therapists describe it as heavy petting—and could easily involve fondling and groping too. Your husband will probably also have been withdrawn and angry or be forever finding fault. It is almost as he's proving to himself that your marriage is so bad that he deserves this "fun" or that his cheating is justified.

What to do: It is really hard to strike the right balance. On one hand, I want to acknowledge that your husband has been restrained enough not to have full sex—by which I mean intercourse, oral sex, or mutual masturbation. On the other hand, I've come across lots of men, and women, who swear blind that it has stopped short of a complete betrayal—only to admit the extent of the infidelity sometimes months and even years later. In addition, lots of spouses find the emotional parts of an affair—sharing time, taking him or her to favorite haunts, or lavishing the care and attention that they have been denied on someone else—more upsetting than the bump-and-grind parts.

Your strategy will depend a lot on whether your husband and the other woman decide to stop or try to justify themselves (I will cover the possibilities later). Whatever happens, please restrain from criticizing the other woman to your husband. I know I'm asking a lot, but you will only encourage him to defend her, sing her praises, or tell you about her troubled life. All you will achieve is to remind him how "special" she is, increase your frustration about his blindness and stupidity and drive you farther apart.

The Full-Blown Affair

As you've probably guessed, this is the full package: emotional and physical infidelity. However, I have male clients who've claimed that it was primarily about sex—although there had been presents and nights out, these have been to facilitate the sex. These men will say, "she meant nothing to me" or "it was just a physical release." Under these circumstances, husbands are normally quick to sever all contact. Although you have the not inconsiderable task of rebuilding your relationship and the fear that he might do it again, at least you're not spending half your time looking over your shoulder and worrying about fresh contact with the other woman.

When the full-blown affair has been sexual as well as emotional, your husband is less likely to come to an immediate decision about whether he wants to stay and fight for your marriage; he might claim that's what he wants, but remain secretly in touch and keep his options open.

What to do: We hate uncertainty and especially if your world has collapsed—this is not an exaggeration after discovering infidelity—you will be desperate to know where you stand. What's more, when you're in pain, you want it to go away—as soon as possible. And when it comes to infidelity, it's excruciating pain. Therefore you will want to act right now, and be able to breathe again, but it is vitally important to avoid trying to solve the problems on the spot.

I am aware that I'm about to repeat myself, but I can't say it too often. Please keep calm. Take deep breaths and then a couple more. I have lots of advice for coping with the drama and madness ahead. However, if you can avoid panicking right now, reaching for magical solutions, or collapsing into a heap on the floor, you will be able to make a proper assessment of the threat posed by the other woman, rather than exaggerating it, and significantly improve the chances of saving your relationship.

There are two scenarios that I particularly want to avoid. Firstly, you are such a quivering heap of jelly that your husband will say anything to make you feel better. Secondly, he's the quivering wreck—racked with guilt and remorse—so you take pity, forgive him, and kiss and make it better.

In the first scenario, he will tell you "I love you and only you" and the other woman "means nothing" and "I will never ever contact her again" and swear it on the health of your children. At that moment in time, he will mean it. 100 percent. I don't have any doubts at all. However, there is a but, a big but. He is trying to appease you. He is trying to assuage his guilt and undo his crime. Except he does not have to face the other woman—yet. She will also be destroyed, because she has been entertaining all sorts of fantasies about happy ever after—and if your husband is like most men who end up in affairs, he will try and appease her too with sneaky emails and a text to check how she is doing. So although you think "it's going to be OK" and he's booking a second honeymoon, in reality, you are being set up for another round of betrayal, discovery, and crisis. Before you know it, your life has descended into a soap opera.

In the second scenario, he is so low and abject that you want to make him feel better. You tell him "I love you," "I'll stand by you," and "We can make this work." He might be able to breath easier, but you've closed down the discussion far too soon. You don't know all the details of the infidelity yet (and he might have done something that is not so easily forgiven), and he has no incentive to be honest (and win you back), because more information about the affair could "spoil things" between the two of you.

So what should you do instead? If it's you who is feeling over-whelmed by emotion during the first few days after discovering your husband's infidelity, ask for a break, a cup of coffee, and perhaps go for a walk to let the news sink in. There will be plenty of opportunity to talk. In fact, you will probably talk more in the next month than you have in the past five years put together. If it's your husband who is breaking down, offer him a drink of water, suggest he takes deep breaths, and tell him "there's no rush." But please don't rescue him.

The rest of the book is focused on coping with uncertainty but, at this point, I have one crucial piece of advice. Don't give ultimatums, such as "it's her or me," or start a ticking clock: "Go away over the weekend and think what you want." Not only does this increase the drama of the crisis, but when you're in shock—and wanting to feel better immediately—neither you nor your husband will make good decisions. Worse still, you're in danger of forcing him to stay—with him subsequently changing his mind, again and again—or throwing him out of the door, only to beg him to return. My goal is for him to choose to stay and for you to decide if that's right for you, your children, and your marriage.

The Love of His Life

This is your worst nightmare. "He never knew what true love meant" and they "were destined to be together" because they are "soul mates." It's enough to make you sick—if you weren't consumed with rejection, anger, and frustration. Under these circumstances, he is determined to leave. He might feel "guilty" and "bad for hurting you," but he's openly seeing her and forever checking his cell phone for her love notes.

What to do: By now, you've probably guessed my answer. Please don't panic. You will think I've taken leave of my senses, but let me explain. Affairs blow up ordinary, mid-range feelings into epic, shout-it-from-the-hills ones. Why should this be?

Excuse me if I state the obvious, but affairs are nasty and deceitful and the fallout can be immense—and in some cases scar lives across generations. Of course, the "lovers" know this, but because nobody wants to be the villain of their own life story, they have to tell themselves—and each other—that they "can't help it," that "this is bigger than both of us," and "I can't live without you." In effect, if you're going to cheat on your wife (or husband), this had better be true love or even better the love match of the century. Throw in the effect of limerence—the crazy part of falling in love—and you feel like a teenager again and able to leap over tall buildings. Details like your children sobbing themselves to sleep are either not registered through the love haze or somehow will be magically sorted. In a nutshell, what I'm saying is that he only thinks she is the love of his life. He doesn't really know her and their relationship has not had to deal with cold hard reality.

What if the someone else is another man?

When some women go through their husband's phone records, they get an extra shock: he's texting or messaging another man, or perhaps a transvestite because this man seems very interested in women's clothing and talks about wearing red lipstick! In most cases, rather than behaving strangely, these husbands have been extra sneaky and put a man's name against his woman's number in order to avoid suspicion. So please don't jump to conclusions.

However, a significant number of wives discover that their husband has had sex with another man. The reaction varies dramatically from woman to woman. Some wives are less hurt by infidelity with a man than another woman, while others fear their whole marriage has been a sham and worry that "he never loved me." In other cases, there is an added complexity when the husband defends himself by claiming, "It's not what you think. I'm not gay!"

If your husband is having sex with another man or you've found him watching gay pornography, you will have a lot to process and many questions. For this reason, I have added an appendix where I answer a couple of women's specific questions and give general advice on how to move forward. However, whoever your husband is texting—man or woman—my general advice still applies and my fight-back plan will still improve communication and help you to talk through the options.

What next?

You have my complete and undivided sympathy. You are going to be tested more than you ever thought possible and feel a range of emotions that you've probably only glimpsed before. The weeks and months ahead are going to be really tough. However, you're going to learn a lot about yourself and these lessons will be useful, whatever happens.

"I have been with my husband for 12 years and married for seven. We have two children aged four years and 21 months. We are both 30 years old. Nine weeks ago, my husband announced he couldn't do it anymore. We were both in our PJs, ready for bed. He just broke down, grabbed some stuff, and then left. We never talked, I was so upset and in shock. He hadn't been right for

months and I had been asking him what was wrong and he dismissed it as he was just a bit down, but didn't know why; then he blamed work and suchlike.

The next night, he called in for some things and went away for two days—to the village where we'd had our honeymoon. On his return, he kept saying he loved me, but didn't know how he loved me (as a partner or just friend). And he needed to see if he missed me. He also announced he wanted his own bank account and was finding somewhere to live. He left again and came back at the weekend, but stayed downstairs—not in our bed.

Three weeks in and he came to stay one Friday night and in the middle of the night he ran away. He heard me dealing with the baby who was crying and he came into the room shaking. He said he needed to get out for a drive around the block, but promised to be back. About 25 minutes later, he rang and told me he was heading back to his friend's couch. I was hysterical and distraught and ended up having a panic attack.

He returned the next morning, as if nothing had happened, but since then didn't attempt to stay again—always saying he felt too anxious or churned up to stay. He would text me every day, during the day and every night when he went to bed. I would ask how he felt and he had up days and down days. Sometimes, he was really positive about our marriage; at others, he was confused. He would come a few times during the week at bath time to see the kids, but would also arrange to come and then move the goal posts at the last minute.

I didn't expect him to come away on vacation, but he did and for four days we had a lovely time. OK, he slept on the couch, but we enjoyed it. On our return I was expecting him to go again, but that night he stayed. He seemed on edge, but I put it down to this anxiety. Then came the killer, a knock at the door about 9 p.m. It was a woman. It turns out he had been having an affair with a girl at work which was where he had been for the last five weeks. He had spent a few nights on the other friend's couch, but he ended up with her.

I was in shock, the whole situation is totally out of character for him. We talked late into the night and he said he had made the decision to stay with us while we were away on vacation. It also transpires that the woman had got his mom's cell phone number from his phone and texted his mom on the first day of our vacation.. His mom, horrified, phoned him, and left a voice-mail having a go at him (she presumed I already knew about the affair, which I didn't). The woman hadn't liked him coming away with us and didn't understand why he wanted to. She was well aware he was texting me every night and morning as he lay in bed with her—which really disturbs me now. He had no idea she was coming that night; he just had a funny feeling she might.

I decided to forgive him. He had been unhappy for a long time and I knew how he felt about me and I could see how it happened—he answered all my questions honestly.

So for the next three weeks, he stayed and we tried, but it was odd toward the last week as he said it didn't feel right being here, then he emailed me to say he didn't want to do this anymore and didn't want us. A few days later he sneakily packed up all his stuff and hid it in his car while I was at the stores. I went to put the ironing away and he stopped me and told me I would find his drawers and closet empty. This again is totally out of character.

He said he had these feelings for her that weren't going away and he couldn't stay. So he went. I let him go. I was too tired to fight anymore and there were so many lies I didn't know what to believe. We texted back and forth that night (he went to a hotel), and I asked did he ever want to fix our marriage? He said he didn't know, but not if it was going to upset me and he knew it would because of how he felt about me. We agreed to be friends; we really are the best of friends and I can't imagine not having him in my life like that.

The next day he returned to take our children swimming. He was still wearing his wedding ring, I had removed mine—as from the previous night, our marriage was well and truly over. He must have noticed as when I looked again his ring had gone. I questioned him and he said he put it on because it didn't occur to him to not put it on that morning, after doing his hair as usual! And with that he took the ring out of his pocket and put it back on his finger! I asked did he want me to put mine back on and he said if I wanted to I could! We had a lovely day, he stayed for coffee, and then left again.

He has found somewhere to rent near where he works. He says he doesn't know how he feels so he isn't giving up on us yet. We spoke again the other day and he says he doesn't want me making any radical plans about anything; the situation isn't bleak, he is trying to be positive.

At the moment, he comes a few times a week to take our daughter to school and collect her, attend swimming lessons, and see me. He wants to stay for tea, do the bath, and bed routine and says he'll happily stay and watch TV with me! I am confused! He says one thing, but his actions do another."

In many ways, what is most upsetting is not knowing from one minute to the next what's going to happen. So let's look at the three possible outcomes and how to fight back.

If he decides to stay

Hurrah! The other woman was more a figment of his imagination, or yours, than a real alternative or when faced with the pain he was causing and the reality of what he'd been doing, your husband has seen sense. You probably felt a wave of euphoria: "It's going to be OK." By all means, enjoy the moment; you have truly earned it. However, this is the moment at which the hard work of repairing your marriage begins. The first task is for your husband to extract himself from his relationship with the other woman.

I know the word "relationship" is upsetting, but it is better to face the truth than to minimize—or conspire with your husband to minimize—what has happened. Even if she was just a Spark, and oblivious of his interest, he needs to organize his life so he sees less of her. If she was an Special Friend, he needs to find a polite way to exit. Even if he had an affair, whether emotional or full-blown, it is best for him to be kind when ending it. I know you will have a low opinion of the other woman. However, in my experience, women enter into affairs because they are deeply unhappy and running away from something painful. So please be compassionate. It will also help you in the long run. If the other woman believes she didn't get a proper explanation or the wife made him do it, she will be more likely to pursue your husband.

Rather than telling your husband how to end the relationship, you need to ask him the following questions:

- What are you going to say to the other woman?

- When?

- How? Face-to-face, by telephone, text?

- How will the other woman react?

- What would help you to extract yourself from this relationship?

- How practical would this plan be?

Here are some questions to discuss together:

- What contact after the exit interview is acceptable?

- What will he do if there is further contact from her?

- If he wants to remain friends, how would this work?

- Can you go from Special Friends to normal friends without a cooling-off period? If so, how long would this need to be? What are the rules, during this period, about contact?

Remember to be assertive and use the formula that I laid out in Part One. *You can ask, he can say no and you can both negotiate.* For example, you could ask "Please sack her." He could say, "No, that's not possible or legal," and you can negotiate. (Perhaps she might agree to join another team so there is less face-to-face contact.) Similarly, he can ask, you can say no and you can both negotiate. For example, he could ask, "Can we still be friends?" You could say, "I don't that's a good idea," and you can both negotiate. Perhaps after six months with no or minimal contact, they could have a proper friendship, which is open to public scrutiny and does not involve sharing secrets—or then again, perhaps not.

If he can't decide

It is horrible to watch someone being racked by indecision or vacillating first one way and then the other. It also plays to all your worst fears: that he doesn't love you, of being not good enough or of abandonment. Meanwhile, the other woman has become more alluring in your imagination and her hold over your husband's heart even stronger.

Having acknowledged both the horror of the situation and the enormity of your fears, it's important to step back and understand why he is unable to make up his mind. Inevitably, it is more complex than at first sight. It could be that he needs a little more time. I know this is tough, but forcing him to make a decision is never a good idea. So discuss the following together:

- What would help him to take stock?

- How practical would that be?

- If he did have time away, how long would it be?

- Where would he go?

- What contact would he have with you?

- What contact would he have with the other woman?

It could be that he's holding things back. Of course, it could be the extent of his feelings for the other woman. However, it is more likely to be the extent of his unhappiness or some criticism of you. In his head, he's thinking, "She's hurting enough without me sticking the knife in too." That's fine, but how can you address the issues if you don't really know the full extent of the problems? So here is how you draw him out.

Firstly, choose your time rather than letting it all come pouring out in the middle of an argument—when anger and frustration will encourage him to exaggerate his criticism of your behavior and amplify his hurt.

Secondly, give him permission to be honest: "I would rather know, so that I can make an informed choice"; "I'm going to be imagining all sorts of horrible things"; or "better out than in."

Thirdly, keep calm and listen (hopefully without getting angry or tearful), and then report back your feelings: "I felt sad when you said ..." In this way, he will treat you as an adult, who has a right to know, rather than a child, who he has to protect.

Finally, he might be having trouble deciding because you're emotionally blackmailing him or he's frightened about how you'll react. Every time he seems to be leaning toward the other woman, do you have a jag of crying, threaten him ("You'll never see the children again"), suggest divorce or get so angry that it closes down the conversation? I know you don't want him to leave. I know you're thinking, "How can we save our marriage if we're not under the same roof?" and you don't want the other woman to win. These are all perfectly valid thoughts, but they are keeping you trapped in limbo; the alternative, letting him leave, is not necessarily all bad.

If he wants to leave

I am not a fan of temporary separations—even if you are regularly meeting up—because it makes it harder to communicate and there are fewer opportunities to work on the relationship by being assertive about day-to-day issues. However, I also want you to listen to your husband and take his opinions seriously. So if he wants to leave, please find out why and discuss his plans.

At this point, you might be able to negotiate a least worst situation, where you have some input into what happens, rather than him just packing his stuff and driving away. I know it will be tough, especially if he is going off to her place or to set up a love nest, but at least everything is out in the open. You don't have to worry that he's secretly in contact with her or have the agony of worrying when he'll be home and what he's been doing. You will not be living in a soap opera.

Fortunately, there is another upside to him leaving. His "true love" will be tested for the first time. Slowly but surely, real life will intrude into his fantasy. He will have to deal with her surly teenage son. She will discover all his nasty habits. They will argue about day-to-day domesticity. It is not exactly Romeo and Juliet. As long as you don't drive them together—by abusive phone calls, being unduly unreasonable about access to the children, and so on—it is highly likely that their relationship will implode.

At this point, your husband will start sending you secret texts. If you're not careful, you can find yourself in the position of being his mistress—which is strange when you're still married. Although the fact that he's sneaking off to have a romantic drink with you will make you feel desired or perhaps seem like cosmic justice, it will not help in the long run and risks a return to soap opera.

My hope is that he will have second thoughts and want to return. If so, discuss the following together:

- How will he know if returning is what he truly wants?

- How can he be certain that he will not bounce back to her again?

- What would be different this time around?

- Are you ready to have him back?

- Would it be a good idea if he went to stay with his parents for a while?

Once the euphoria of coming home has worn off, you will still need to work on the issues that undermined your relationship before the other woman arrived on the scene.

Love Coach's Three Key Things to Remember

- Keep calm and don't make decisions that will help you feel better today but set up more problems for tomorrow.

- Aim to be polite and solicitous about your husband's welfare, but don't try to solve his problems for him.

- Once the immediate shock of discovering infidelity has passed, if your life is resembling a soap opera that's probably a sign that you need a fresh approach to resolving this crisis.

CHAPTER EIGHT

He says one thing
but his actions say another

"I've been dealt another blow just three months into our reconciliation after my husband's affair. I just had an odd feeling, so I logged onto his email account and discovered that he'd registered with an online dating website. None of the messages were anything more than just chatting. When I confronted him, he initially denied it. Then he just said that he was curious and that it never would have gone any further. He then proceeded to curl up into the fetal position and say that he has always made a mess of everything in his life. I told him I wasn't interested in his self-pity and he got very angry. He started shouting and shaking, saying that he has every right to be as angry as I am. I was completely dumbfounded.

I kicked him out and destroyed all of our wedding photos and my engagement and wedding rings have gone out with the garbage (the trash was collected yesterday and I am actually pretty devastated).

He came back later in the evening, adamant that he has meant everything he has said and done throughout our reconciliation and has no idea why he registered with this site. He is also adamant he still loves me and has never wanted a future with anyone else, but how can I ever believe him?'

You might imagine there's nothing worse than discovering your husband is texting someone else. Unfortunately, there is a lower level of hell. You confront him about his behavior, but after lots of tears and recriminations, he begs for forgiveness and you agree to try and save your marriage. So far, so good. It seems as if you're making good progress, except suddenly you find even *more* evidence of his lying and cheating. It could be something else about his past infidelity (for example he'd been seeing two women, not one), even though he's sworn that he's told you everything. It might be fresh crimes—like more contact with his "friend" or joining an adult website. It seems that before you've had a chance properly to pick yourself up from the first set of discoveries, that he's kicked you in the stomach—again and again. Worse still, he can't explain why he's been so stupid. He claims that he loves you and wants only you and the children, but his actions say the complete opposite. Why can't he just be straight with you?

Six reasons why your husband's behavior makes no sense

In the first hours and days after the fresh discovery, your husband will probably be in shock. Of course, he knew his behavior was wrong and is going to set back your recovery, but he minimized his actions to himself ("I was only looking" or "it was only one text"), excused himself ("I was going to tell you that she'd been around to my office, but I hadn't found the right time yet") and put everything into a separate, watertight compartment, in order that what happens in one area of his life or on the internet has no impact on the rest. So when he is confronted by the full extent of his deception or the pain it's causing you, he can't quite believe that he's been so stupid. However, even when the shock has worn off, he still can't explain why he's kept information back or slipped back into his old ways and sabotaged what he says he wants. In my experience, it's down to six possible reasons.

He doesn't have the tools

As I explained in Part One, men are brought up to act, rather than to examine their feelings. In many cases, they have bought the prevailing cultural messages from Hollywood, popular TV, and thriller novels that showing your feelings is a sign of weakness. It is only a short step from this to believing feelings are a handicap or, at the very least, an inconvenience and therefore best denied, suppressed, or intellectualized into submission. So it comes as a complete revelation to men when I explain that they need to be able to name and understand their feelings, because they are clues to how to make a wise decision.

Their wives are often open-mouthed and ask if he really does need to be taught how to feel. Of course not, but some men need permission to listen to their feelings and work out the complex brew of emotions bubbling under the surface—rather than being ambushed by them and then either walking away or simply getting angry.

If ever there was a time when your husband needed to be "in touch"' with his feelings, it is now. Unfortunately, he simply does not have the tools or training. In effect, it is a bit like putting someone behind the wheel of a car for the first time and pointing them in the direction of a freeway at rush hour. There is bound to be a crash and people will get hurt.

Turn it around: Unfortunately, some women unwittingly reinforce the stereotyping when men do break down or complain and effectively tell them to "man up." You probably don't use that phrase, but your actions might send that message. For example, according to the letter that opens this chapter, when the man is curled up in a ball the woman tells him to "lose the self-pity." In effect, she is sabotaging her goal of getting him to open up because she is uncomfortable with the feelings that emerge.

So what's the alternative? I know this a big ask—because you're under immense stress too—but I would like you to model what he should be doing. Firstly, acknowledging the feeling and, secondly, naming it. So for example: "I know this is difficult or painful or overwhelming," or "you're feeling guilty and angry with yourself." If you just stick with it, rather than trying to rescue or attack him, and sit with him and witness these difficult emotions, he will slowly but surely calm down and you can begin to talk; then you can tell him about your feelings too.

Time and again, when men open up, it's a bit like the Pandora's box of Greek myth. The first feelings to escape are often negative, but once they have been expressed, you will find hope, more balanced emotions, and with luck, love.

He's lying to himself

One of the great problems with infidelity, beyond the pain it causes everybody, is the lies. You might start off lying to your partner to facilitate the affair, but you will always end up lying to yourself too. Perhaps the idea is best expressed by the nine-teenth-century author Fyodor Dostoevsky (1821–1881) in his novel *The Brothers Karamazov*: "Above all, do not lie to yourself. The man who lies to himself and listens to his own lie comes to such a pass that he cannot distinguish the truth within himself."

> *Perhaps it starts off as a white lie to keep the peace at home, for example "It doesn't matter that my wife and I don't have much sex." However, the underlying resentment does not go away. Slowly, the lies get bigger and a little grayer: "What's the harm in going out for a couple of drinks with a work colleague?" Before too long, they are outright lies, such as "I have to work late," and not just to you, but the other woman too. For example, he may say "I'm not married," but he fails to mention that he's been liv-ing with someone for fifteen years and they have two children together.*

In effect, if your husband is routinely lying to himself and the two people whom he professes to love or have feelings for, how can he begin to know what he wants?

Turn it around: Take everything he says with a huge pinch of salt—both the horrible stuff ("I hate you") and the nice stuff ("I will do anything to save our marriage"). After all, how can he know what he feels when he cannot be honest with himself? Although it is difficult to live with the uncertainty, it is better than putting pressure on yourself to believe him, and being con-stantly let down, or swallowing his negative messages wholesale and turning a crisis into a catastrophe.

He's a people-pleaser

I'm struck by how often men who get themselves into this mess are described as great husbands and fathers by their wives. How-ever, it is easy to slip from being a good man who is kind and considerate to others into a people-pleaser, who will go to any lengths to make others happy and avoid conflict—thereby denying his own needs and not being kind or considerate to himself. You can ignore your own needs only so long before you snap and think, "I deserve this ..." or even, "I need this to keep my sanity."

Often the other woman will pose as someone with no needs; she certainly doesn't need him to pick up the kids from a friend's birthday party, the dry cleaning from the other side of town, and more toilet rolls if he's just passing the grocery store. So it is easy for a people-pleasing man to think that he can have something just for himself for once. However, once he is in this new relationship, he will find that this woman has just as many needs as everyone else. She really needs him to call. She really needs to see him. She really needs to feel special and wanted. Bearing in mind that his default position is people-pleasing, he will go out of his way to meet these needs. He will also be people-pleasing at work too—so he can't say no when his boss dumps a pile of work on his desk. Before too long, he's trying to keep the plates spinning at home, at work, and in affair-land. As you can imagine, it is impossible without increasingly wild lies and his life descending first into farce and then tragedy.

So although he might agree to no contact with the other woman, because he's a nice guy and wants to make things better, he's equally susceptible to her email to his work account saying, "I can't move on without a proper explanation." And before he has thought it through, he's off for a clandestine cup of coffee.

Turn it around: It is easy to take this behavior very personally. After all, he can't be straight with you! However, the behavior goes back a very long way. In fact, I would be prepared to stake large sums on him appeasing his mother when he was a little boy and, even today, he'll do anything to keep her sweet.

Hopefully, you will have started to follow the advice in Part One and become assertive (rather than domineering or swinging between passive and domineering), and your changes will have helped him to become more assertive too. When you find out about the next secret text or rendezvous, don't jump to conclusions such as "he loves her more than me," "he can't live without her," or "she'll always be in our lives." Tell yourself that he's a people-pleaser; what else would he do? Hopefully, it will keep you calm enough to listen to his explanation and make a proper assessment of the damage. More times than not, the discoverer blows these events into a huge set back when it is more likely to be a stumble—because it is hard to go from being a people-pleaser to being assertive overnight. There will be set backs, but it doesn't have to be the end of your relationship—unless you want it to be.

Modern technology

The instant nature of modern communication means that it is easy to type first and think second. Worse still, these messages can be retrieved even months later and minutely dissected. So even a passing whim or fleeting feeling has the impression of being lasting and unchanging. If that wasn't bad enough, words may be taken out of context and interpreted in a million different ways. I am a professional and have spent many years learning and honing my craft. I write and rewrite and I still get misquoted, misunderstood, and surprised by the conclusions people sometimes draw from my books.

When we're face to face, the tone of our voices, and our body language are far more important than the words used, so when you try to interpret your husband's texts and emails to the other woman you have only a few fragments of the total message and no context. No wonder nothing makes sense.

Turn it around: Most couples could benefit from a rethink about what I call smartphone etiquette. We are tethered to our phones and "on call" almost 24/7, but what message does this give our partner if we break off our conversation to read a text or we're busy tweeting while watching TV together? In a nutshell, it says that there is somebody more important or more interesting than you. It also means that anybody—without an invitation—can wander into your house.

When your marriage is under strain, it is doubly important to have boundaries between what is acceptable smartphone behav-

ior and what isn't. Every couple will come to a different conclusion, but here are a few ideas. Switch off your phones while having a meal together. Don't have your smartphones on in the bedroom—that is your private space. You could always buy a dedicated alarm clock, rather than use the phone alarm. Have a curfew time for all smartphone or internet activity. One of the main reasons we're facing a sleepless epidemic is because we are not giving our brains enough time to wind down before going to bed. Experts suggest at least an hour and a half. If you suddenly remember something that needs to be done, make a note and do it in the morning.

If you're going further—especially after an internet affair—and have decided that looking at social networking sites is forbidden or severely curtailed, remember that for rules to stick they need to apply to everybody; so don't ban your partner from the internet in the evening while you're happily instant-messaging friends and on auction sites selling unwanted clothes.

Shame

Shame is the most toxic of emotions and something we will do almost anything to escape. At this point, you're probably thinking that if he feels shame for what he's done, that's all well and good, perhaps he won't do it again! However, shame is far more complex than that. Picture a small kid, standing on the table, and their mother or father comes into the room. Of course, the parents tell them off, because they don't want them to fall and hurt themselves. Unfortunately, it can easily come out as "you're a naughty boy (or girl)," rather than as "you're doing something naughty." And that's the problem, especially if our parents used shaming a lot: it gives the message that we are unlovable (as people) rather than simply doing something that displeases (our behavior). As you can imagine, nobody wants to be unlovable or to be cast out into the darkness—the pain is unbearable—so we try to lessen the shame with one of three tactics:

- *Justifying ourselves.* In effect, we try to diminish the crime, "I was only looking"; normalize it, "everybody does it"; or rationalize it, "I thought it would help."

- *Going on the attack.* In effect, we try to push the shame onto the other person: "You shouldn't check up on me"; "You're so controlling"; or "Have you ever thought why I might …"

- *Closing down.* The pain is so great that we walk away or climb into our shells and shut out the world.

As you can imagine, none of these tactics really helps to resolve the situation. When your husband justifies unacceptable behavior, it makes you angry and increases your criticism, which shames him more. When he goes on the attack, you either withdraw yourself, and your husband feels slightly better, or fight back and increase the levels of shame. Your husband closing down can lower the temperature, but it also encourages you to up the ante, and shame him even more, or, in some cases that I have counseled, the woman has even become violent—in a misguided attempt to break through her husband's defenses and communicate—and ends up feeling shame herself. Instead of the shame going away, it builds and builds and becomes more and more toxic.

Ultimately, your husband will become so overwhelmed by shame and self-loathing that he'll need to block out the pain—immediately. So guess what he does? He goes online to flirt with random women—who by showing interest prove that he is not completely unlovable—or texts the other woman, who will help him to justify his behavior ("It's real love") or attack you ("How can she say those things about you?") and generally tell him he's wonderful. Alternatively, he will get drunk, which lowers his inhibitions and makes him more likely to misbehave, use street drugs, or sink farther into depression. Guess what? He ends up feeling even more shame and his behavior gets even worse.

So what are the long-term effects of this cycle of shame? You could really and truly believe that your husband is a bad person, rather than just doing bad things, and divorce slowly but surely becomes inevitable. Meanwhile, your husband thinks you're permanently angry, rather than angry about certain deeds, and who wants to be married to someone like that?

Turn it around: It is important to keep your criticism specific and targeted at his behavior. That's why I recommend reporting your feelings (see Chapter Four, pages 78–80), using this formula:

> *I feel …*
> *when you …*
> *because …*

The first part, *I feel …*, avoids misunderstanding. He thinks it's anger when it's really disappointment or maybe despair. The second part, *when you …*, targets the feelings to a specific time—rather than always or constantly—and the third part, *because …*, explains why it hurts so much. It is a good idea to follow up with some reassurance, such as "It's not that I think you're a bad man," or "I want to love you, but you're making it hard." Most importantly, it will stop you from getting trapped in the downward spiral of shame—where your reaction does not prevent further hurtful actions, but prompts more of the same.

Fear

Your husband is dealing with multiple, overlapping, and competing fears. He's frightened that your relationship will never get any better. He's frightened that he will sink into depression or farther into depression and despair. He's frightened that he's going to crack up. He's frightened of losing you. He's frightened of hurting you even more by staying. He's frightened of damaging the kids or alienating them or of you turning them against him. He's frightened about what his mother and father will think and of the opinions of people in general. He's frightened that this other woman might possibly be his savior and he's going to let her walk away. He's frightened that she won't save him, but is actually going to pull him under. He's frightened about how all this is affecting his work and his ability to pay the bills. He's frightened that he's a bad man. He's frightened of making the biggest mistake of his life. I could go on, but I think I've made my point.

You'll probably wonder why he doesn't stop running and simply face his fears. It's a good question, but you're dealing with someone who has been trained to ignore his feelings—except when they completely overwhelm him and he's got no choice but to react and that seldom leads to good decision-making. More importantly, owning up to being frightened (even to himself) is a sign of weakness and a weak man is hardly a man at all.

Furthermore, when someone is frightened of making a mistake they will try to keep their options open. In effect, they kick the can farther down the road in the hope that something will change, someone else will decide for them or their feelings might become clearer.

Turn it around: The problem is that you're frightened too and, when you're fearful, it is easy to lash out, make threats (which you might not necessarily mean), and add to his mountain of fear. For example,: "If you don't shape up, I'm out of here," or "I'm going to go online too and find someone who'll make me feel special." Of course, it's all right to express your fears when you're calm, he can listen, and you can have a sensible discussion. However, hurling threats when you're angry is just going to make things worse. Try to remember that he's just as frightened as you are and if you can find common ground—by acknowledging that you're both in the same place—you're laying the foundations for tackling this problem as a team.

Making a plan

So you've discovered an affair, more evidence about your husband's past infidelity, or continuing contact with the other woman. I hope my insight into your husband's behavior has helped to take the edge off your panic and that you're ready to talk about moving forward:

> *"Four months ago, I discovered that my husband was having an affair at work with a married woman and mother of two. It was difficult for them to find times when they could be alone, they mostly interacted via daily emails or texts, but they also met several times secretly and had close physical contact, but no sex.*

However, I can't help feeling they would have probably taken things further if I hadn't discovered the affair so soon.

A few days after being discovered, my husband told me that he had agreed with his lover to revert their interactions to friendship. They would still have an occasional lunch together at work and maintained sporadic contact by email and text. I was tolerating their behavior because I could imagine how hard, if not impossible, it would have been for them to stop communicating abruptly right after the discovery. I wanted them to have time to accept the idea that it was over and come to their senses.

Six weeks later, they were still in touch. I came home one day to the smell of burned dinner. I asked him if he had been emailing his lover, which he confirmed, but he said just as friends. I believed that this was his intent, but couldn't help thinking that he was trying to fool himself. On the same evening I told him I was OK with them being in touch, but asked if he could be honest with me and let me know when and why it occurred (but without having to go further into detail about it).

My husband did not react well to the idea, taking this as a proof of my mistrust and me wanting to control him. I got a little desperate at this stage because I thought I had been extremely understanding, letting them be in touch after the discovery. We were completely at odds with how we were seeing things. Even if I had not voiced it, I was expecting him to sever communications with her eventually. However, he thought that there was nothing wrong with them staying in touch, that it would be like being in contact with an ex.

Eventually, two days later, he told me that he had asked his lover to stop emailing, texting, and calling him, that he had found it very hard to do this to her, but he could see that it would mean a lot to me. But that he might want to reestablish contact later when things would settle down between us. I am so worried that he will let himself be consumed again into their internet interactions and start up the affair again."

It is extremely hard to know what to do after discovering your husband is texting, or still texting, another woman. You want her out of your life, so you can have space to work on your marriage and begin to feel safe again. However, your husband is minimizing the impact of their continuing contact, trying to hide behind being "friends," and generally putting his head in the sand. So it is very tempting to take the initiative, lay down the law, and say "no contact." I have a lot of sympathy for this approach, but over and over again I've seen it backfire for the following reasons:

The "friends" have feelings for each other

Although their 'connection' is probably based on fantasy, wishful thinking, and exaggeration, it still feels incredibly good, and your husband and the other woman will find it hard to go cold turkey—I use that phrase advisedly. Your husband has been self-medicating his unhappiness with attention from another woman or he feels good about himself because he's rescuing her from her miserable existence. If you cut off his "supply,", of course he'll have withdrawal symptoms and crave another hit—especially since his supplier (the other woman) is tempting him or playing on his sense of guilt about abandoning her.

You can't make anyone do anything

Staying with the drug rehab analogy, your husband has to want to give up contact, rather than be ordered to or made to feel so guilty that he acquiesces—at least to your face. Worse still, you become the law enforcement and start checking and double-checking. No wonder you're on edge all the time and he feels distrusted. It goes without saying that this is not a good environment for working on your relationship.

You're setting yourself up for failure

If you can't impose a solution without consent, you're going to end up looking stupid, because your impotence is staring you straight in the face; blowing your top, which brings us back to the shame trap; and making threats, which you don't carry through because you're terrified of losing him. In effect, you're turning a crisis into a catastrophe and risk getting to the point where you'll believe your marriage is past saving.

It's domineering rather than assertive

Of course you want this affair to be over, but there is a big gap between asking for no contact and laying down the law. Remember my formula for good communication: You can ask. He can say no and you can negotiate. In this way, you can avoid being controlling (who wants to be in a relationship with a controlling partner?) and, at the same time, lay the foundations for a plan that works for both of you.

Seven tips for negotiating a workable solution

Most people find negotiation really hard. Asking for what we want seems dangerous, because we're frightened of being rejected. Saying no is fraught with difficulty, because we're worried that our beloved won't love us unless we agree with him or her—and doubly so at such a moment, because we're terrified that the loved one will walk out the door.

Therefore, we much prefer to buy into the myth that if "he really loved me, he'd want to make me happy …" But that comes with a dark side: "If he won't, it means he doesn't love me." So let me offer some reassurance: it is perfectly possible to love someone and disagree with them—that's where negotiation comes in.

Take your time

Although you will want to feel better immediately, I would avoid trying to set up a plan in the aftermath of discovery. You will both be in shock, feeling upset and guilty. None of these emotions makes for a calm survey of the problem or a lasting solution. It is much better to negotiate after the dust has settled a little. So please feel free to take a rain check: for example "I can't think straight at the moment"; "I've been overwhelmed with competing feelings"; and "Can we talk about this again when I've had a chance to reflect?"

Let solutions emerge

Rather than going in with a plan or a preferred solution, start with an open mind. In this way, you won't fall into the trap of trying to impose your choice, and being so busy defending your position that you can't truly listen to your partner.

Ask questions rather than describe the problem

It is very easy to spend more time explaining your distress and your fears than trying to find a solution. If you're feeling stuck, ask a question, such as "what are we going to do about it? or where do we go from here?."

Don't dismiss any plan, however ludicrous

Your husband might make a suggestion that gets your heart racing, for example, "I will wean her off me bit by bit." Instead of dismissing it outright, which will get his back up, ask more questions: "How will that work?"; "How do you think I will feel?"; "How long will that take?" This approach will provide insight into what your husband is thinking, and sometimes even a poor suggestion may be the springboard for something positive, so keep the dialogue open and enquiring.

Make the plan explicit

By this I mean spelling out what is suggested, rather than one or both of you assuming something—and getting upset at a later date because it was not what you expected. For example, if he is going to have time away to straighten his head, what contact will there be with you or with the other woman? If she phones and begs to meet up during his "thinking time," what will he do? Where he is going to stay? Rather than assuming, ask a question. By this point, you should be beginning to outline some rules of engagement. Instead of hoping your husband will know what you expect, make it explicit. After all, under the rules of assertiveness, you can ask, he can say no, and you can have a further round of negotiation.

Double-check

Go back over the plan and look at whether it is practical. Although while he is sitting at your kitchen table, staring into your eyes, and holding your hand, your husband might be resolved, for example, to cut her dead, how will that work out if they are currently working on a project together? If you have doubts, please express them. If possible, frame these as questions rather than accusations. For example: say "How will you deal with site meetings?" rather than "You won't be able to keep your hands off each other." Remember, assertiveness is based on equal rights, so please give him the opportunity to express his doubts too. Once again, it is better to find potential holes at this point and try to plug them, rather than rushing forward on a wave of euphoria.

Sleep on it

I often counsel women who lose sight of their own needs because they are so determined to save their relationship and are therefore fixed on what is best for their husband—because if he can feel better, then the marriage will be better, and then she will feel better. In the worst cases, they agree to plans that are destructive, not only to her peace of mind but to her sanity and even her love for her husband. That's why I always suggest sleeping on a plan so you have space to think. It is better to tell your husband that you're having second thoughts, and start negotiating again, rather than pressing on against your better judgment.

What is a friend?

Some negotiations get derailed because a husband will agree to stop having sex with the other woman, but wants them still to be "friends," claims he needs contact—at least for the time being—or that their flirty texting is harmless.

"I found out that my husband was texting a girl from work excessively all day. The next day I confronted him and he said, 'Don't worry, she is, like, 500 pounds and ugly.' I showed him the evidence on Facebook that she is thin and attractive. He said, 'Babe, she is just a friend; I would love it if you met her because you would like her.' I said if there is nothing going on, then why would you lie about her weight? He said it was because, in the past six months, I've acted jealous and he was afraid if I knew she was

159

attractive in any way he would have to stop being friends. So I bought the story and let him continue texting her.

Finally, I was able to sneak a view at his phone and I found 'I want to be close to you and know you better than anyone' and that he had told her all of our relationship problems. I confronted my husband again and he swears he has always had female friends like this, is madly in love with me, and just needed someone to talk to while I'm unavailable dealing with our son (who is in and out of hospital with a life-threatening illness).

Is it possible for married women and men to have opposite-sex friends who are this close?"

So what are the boundaries and when does a friendship become inappropriate? In my opinion, there are five differences.

- *Real friendships are open to public scrutiny.* Friendship does not happen in secret and the friends do not have to lie to themselves or anyone else about the amount of contact.

- *Real friends socialize with each other's partners.* It is fine to have friends where the majority of your contact does not involve your partner. However, when you have bigger social events— like a birthday party—you should be able to invite all your friends or, from time to time, make up a foursome with your partner, your friend, and his or her significant other.

- *Real friends do not have that much social contact.* Although I don't want to make sweeping generalizations, most men contact their friends only occasionally; in some cases they can have long-term friendships based on sporadic contact, where sometimes months or even years pass without speaking or meeting up. Even if they do have close female friends, they seldom speak or have an extended text chat more than once or twice a week.

- *Real friendships does not involve betraying secrets.* Although you may ask for advice or a second opinion from friends, you do not give intimate details of problems or bond by sharing confidences.

- *Real friends do not flirt.* This is especially true of friendships between heterosexual men and women—which are based on shared interests, such as work or a hobby, or frequent contact, as friends of their partner—because they are aware of the damage that straying into sexually charged territory would bring. Sometimes when one friend is gay, there can be explicitly sexual flirting, but the interaction stays safe because neither party expects the other to follow through.

I am sure that you instinctively know where the boundaries lie, but I find it is necessary to lay down the differences between appropriate and inappropriate friends—if only in your own head—because a particularly articulate or stubborn man can make you question your own judgment. Please don't get drawn into a debate about the rights and wrongs of their friendship—it will just make you furious and build a wall between the two of you; instead, try asking a few questions.

- *If she is a friend, when can I meet her?* It's not that you want to be part of their every interaction, but if she is truly a friend, he will want to introduce her to you.

- *Why can't you text, email, or talk to me?* You would love even a quarter of the attention that this woman is getting. So ask him what's stopping him from contacting you?

- *Do you need to speak to a professional?* If he needs to talk to her because she is, for example, helping him with work problems or to deal with stress, what are her qualifications for this role? Would he be better speaking to his doctor, human resources at work, or a therapist?

- *How will you move from being "special" friends one day to a normal friendship the next?* I am not certain how this can be done (it normally requires a period of limited or no contact), but perhaps your husband has a suggestion. Listen to him and ask questions, rather than shooting him down.

- *What impact is this friendship having on our relationship?* Obviously, you know the answer to this one! However, getting him to think about it—rather than you telling him—might make him consider the issues, and perhaps even come to a similar conclusion to you.

What if we're still stuck?

Don't be surprised if there are setbacks and failures. Tell yourself that it is part of the process, rather than your relationship is doomed. Ask yourself what you both can learn from this hiccup and how you can both improve on your plan. In the following chapters, I will explain how to deal with the other woman and your own panic. In the meantime, practice being assertive, rather than passive (agreeing to anything to keep him) or domineering (telling him how it's going to be). Remember, it will take time to sort out a workable solution.

Love Coach's Three Key Things to Remember

- Your husband's behavior will be unpredictable. He's under immense pressure and he does not have the tools to understand or process his feelings and therefore to make sensible decisions.

- Shaming your husband might make you feel temporarily better, but you risk pushing him so far down that, in an effort to feel better, he will indulge in more unhelpful behavior.

- You can't control your husband, but you can ask for what you need, listen to him, and negotiate.

CHAPTER NINE

Why can't the other woman just leave him alone?

"I began flirting with men, to get attention (I think), and because marriage was not what I had expected, and I felt severe anxiety about being with only one person for the rest of my life. Pretty soon I found myself in a very bad situation with one man that I had led on. He showed up on my doorstep and I felt that I had led him on enough that I needed to 'follow through.' We slept together and it was horrible. It was awkward, shameful, guilt-ridden, you name it. I felt disgraceful. Yet when he came back the next day ... I decided after the second time that I had to come clean with my husband and that it could NEVER happen again. I told him everything and, after a long night of talking, he decided to forgive me. However, he wanted to 'forget about it and never deal with it again.' I knew it was wrong, but felt I needed to let him heal in whatever way he needed.

Weeks and months went by and he withdrew from me and we lost our emotional connection completely. Over time, I still felt the strong urge to flirt, but I knew I could never let it get physical again. So I found myself talking to strangers in chat rooms and sending them inappropriate pictures of myself. I loved the thrill of turning someone on and of them desiring my body. It became an addiction. I started sending them to people I knew, not just strangers. I began emailing old boyfriends, current friends, and so on. I sent pictures, exchanged fantasies, but never let it get physical again.

My husband and I started a family and, shortly after the birth of our first child, I began to feel depressed about my weight gain. Motherhood wasn't what I had expected either, and I fell into a depression. After losing some weight and feeling good about myself again, I went right back into my addiction of talking to others. My husband found the emails and actually confronted the men, rather than me. When they retreated and stopped emailing me back, I felt rejected and begged them to keep talking to me. He read each and every word of my telling these men how much I 'needed' them, but I had no idea he was reading them. He finally confronted me and told me he knew everything. He begged me to stop and told me I was ruining our family. I tried and succeeded for a while. After the birth of our second child, we drifted farther apart. He became addicted to his work and exercise, often choosing those things over us. I felt neglected and alone, and resorted to texting/emailing again."

I have included this letter from a wife who compulsively chased other women's husbands to give you an insight into your husband's "friend," "lover," or whatever he wants to call her. You're probably thinking that, for example, she's younger than you, she hasn't had three children (so must have a better figure), or that life with her would be fun and carefree. Meanwhile, you're feeling worn out, worthless, and cast aside with all the boring responsibilities. So it follows that she must be "better" than you and that your husband and this other woman must have a "special" connection.

However, as this letter shows, your rival is most probably fundamentally unhappy, riddled with self doubt, and trying to solve a mountain of problems of her own. As I always say to my clients, "She must be in a pretty dark place, if she thinks another woman's husband is going to save her, and completely deluded if she imagines life with fractious stepchildren is going to be a walk in the park."

In all likelihood, your husband and the other woman's "special connection" is based on mutual neediness and that's no foundation for happy ever after.

Why she won't let go

The exact reasons will change from woman to woman, the nature of her relationship with your husband and his behavior, but these are the most common factors driving her on—even though your husband has ended it or tried to end it several times.

She hasn't had a "proper explanation"

In the bubble of their flirtation or affair, he has probably told her that she is the light of his life, that just being with her gives his life meaning and shape, and that their love will conquer all obstacles. With this in mind, being told that his wife has found out and it's got to stop or that he's giving his marriage another try will make no sense at all.

She is also struggling with a problem that I see a lot. We imagine that if only we can understand then we can move on and put the pain behind us. I have a lot of time for this idea, but it is true only up to a point. Of course understanding helps, but we still have to grieve as well, because nothing can simply magic pain away.

In addition, if she is looking for an explanation from your husband, she will probably be disappointed and frustrated. As you've discovered, he has not been trained to look at or listen to his feelings and therefore has limited personal insight.

She is mourning

Losing something precious—even if based on fantasy—is hard and so we need to mourn. However, this involves looking back over what happened, trying to make sense of events, and wondering what you could or should have done differently. As you can imagine, the person that you've lost is on your mind a lot. However, most people don't recognize that dwelling on the past is a natural part of the grieving process, rather than a sign that "you really love him" or "you should be together." No wonder she is tempted to text and "see how he's doing" or to beg more blatantly for another chance. After all, she's come up with a thousand things she could do differently—because thinking "what if" is another part of the grieving process too.

Her life is chaotic

She entered into an affair or distracted herself with a flirtation because she was unhappy and wanted to feel better. As I've pointed out, time and time again, affairs don't solve problems, rather they add lots of new ones to the pile. So she's not only hurting from the split or frightened of losing her savior, but also facing the cold, hard reality of her old life. Although I would like to think she would start trying to sort out the original problems, it is difficult to do when you're down, depressed, and overwhelmed. It is far easier to believe in the "power of love," which brings me to the next reason.

She believes in soul mates

As you know, I am dubious about this idea and even more dubious whether you can be soul mates when you have been systematically lying—or simplifying the truth. Since love has saved her, or appeared to, from her problems beforehand, she is certain she will feel better if she just hears his voice and, if he meant what he said—which he must because the alternative is too horrible then he will want to hear from her too.

She is getting encouragement from your husband

Your husband is going through a similar mourning process and mistaking thinking about someone for proof that they belong together. If you're giving him the message "I hate you: don't leave me" or are sometimes consumed with anger (which might be justified, but makes him feel hopeless), he might try to keep his options open. He could also have black and white ideas about love, such as "it shouldn't be this hard," so when the two of you have a setback, for example a terrible row, he will lose faith in working on your relationship and medicate his despair with a sneaky text to her.

Alternatively, she might interpret his acts of kindness—not cutting her completely dead in the street or getting her a cup of coffee at work—as a sign of hope and, if she's in a truly dark place, it is easy to build even the tiniest glimmer into a shining beacon.

She thinks you're a witch

Everybody needs to be the hero of their own life and if you're stopping her from being happy, then you'll have been cast in the role of the baddie. In other words, you're an evil witch who is casting a spell over her beloved and she has to save him from you. Once she's reached this point, any behavior—throwing you into a cauldron of boiling water or getting blackbirds to peck out your eyes—is justifiable.

Magical thinking

Although all the previous reasons are important, this is perhaps the key reason she is still pursuing your husband against all the odds. So what do I mean by magical thinking? Change is difficult. It takes time. There are setbacks. And it involves looking deeply into corners of our personality and behavior that we'd rather not face.

Therefore, it is easier to clutch at some small event or minor change and believe it will throw a switch and everything will be fine. So an example of magical thinking would be: "If we could just meet up, we will find a way of resolving the fact that we're both married, have six children between us, no money, and live in different countries." Alternatively: "If I drove past his house, he might see me, know how much I cared, and come outside." In the cold light of day, it all seems a bit preposterous, but when we're desperate it is easy to clutch at a magical solution. However, the alternative, of facing a mountain of problems and slowly climbing over them, seems even more impossible. So what happens? We discard one magical solution and come up with another to take its place.

What you can learn from the other woman

I wonder if you experienced some uncomfortable feelings as you read through the previous section? Did any of the traps seem horribly familiar? Sometimes it is easier to spot unhelpful behavior or thinking in someone else, so let's go back over these points and see if you're making any of the same mistakes.

- Do you believe that if you could really understand why your husband has been texting another woman you'd feel somehow better? Is that why you keep pushing him for answers— even though his replies don't make sense and cause unnecessary arguments? Are you hoping to magic the pain away?

- Do you need to mourn? Not necessarily for your marriage, but for the relationship that you thought you had. Many women talk about how their dreams were shattered and how they now look at their husband through realistic, rather than rose-tinted, glasses and how their marriage used to be "innocent." Hopefully, you're moving toward a truer version of love, rather than one based on a fairy-tale version of love. However, you do need to let go of the old relationship before you can move forward.

- Do you need to update your ideas about love? Although the fantasy of finding The One, settling down, and living happily ever after is powerful and comforting, it leaves you profoundly vulnerable if your husband says, "I don't love you anymore." On the other hand, my vision of love, which combines chemistry and the tools to feed and tend your connection, might be less "magical" but it is more empowering.

- Have you turned the other woman into a cartoon too? Perhaps you see her as a Jessica Rabbit figure (all alluring curves and long legs) or maybe a cheap whore (who just services men). The first version will invest her with powers she most probably does not possess and the second paints her as someone without feelings and seriously underestimates her.

- Have you been guilty of magical thinking? Have you been promoting something, like a vacation away with the kids, because, in your mind, it will be the breakthrough or he'll remember how good you are together and everything will then be magically sorted? Have you been blind to the damage your persistence has caused—because the ends justify the means? Have you felt hopeless and full of despair when the desired outcome was not achieved? Had you, in effect, set up an arbitrary test for your relationship which it subsequently failed— even though, for example, it's perfectly possible for the other woman to sabotage a "makeup" vacation—but it doesn't mean your relationship is doomed?

Should I confront the other woman?

This is a complex issue, because in doing this some wives have made a difficult situation worse, while others have learned a lot from the encounter:

"Even after I had confronted my husband about his inappropriate relationship with another woman, he continued the contact with her on and off for two years. During this time, I repeatedly confronted him about it and each time he promised to stop. I made it clear that our marriage stood no hope of being rebuilt with a third person diverting his emotional energy and commitment— yet still it continued. I tried hard to understand the reason for the relationship, but my husband would never tell me anything, other than saying that it was flirting that had got out of control and it would stop if things were OK between us.

One evening I discovered they had once again met up and I decided enough was enough and that I needed to speak to the woman, as the message didn't seem to be getting through to my husband. I needed to understand why they were behaving in this way—risking both of their marriages; what did they have that stopped them letting go? I also wanted to tell her that if the contact didn't stop, I would speak to her husband—I needed to feel I wasn't completely powerless. I let my rage subside for a couple of days, then surprised her at her workplace. Her shock and fear at seeing me gave me an immediate sense of satisfaction in return for the pain she had caused me.

I was extremely calm and gave her time to explain what had been going on. The meeting lasted 30 minutes and afterward I felt a huge sense of peace and release. I had met this previously 'unknown' woman and all my anxieties about my husband having found the 'ideal' woman were unfounded. She wasn't any more attractive than me and, frankly, seemed very insecure and self-orientated. I was reassured that she had no deep feelings for my husband, as she was very quick to point the finger of blame at him and justified her behavior on the basis that her own marriage was struggling, she was ambitious and therefore welcomed the attention from her boss.

As much as she provided a sense of escape for my husband, she also represented a huge, demonlike figure in my mind, always making me question why I wasn't good enough anymore to be my husband's special woman—was it my age, looks, conversation? That demon was exorcised from my mind the day I met her. This left me feeling back in control and relieved that there was one less obstacle to rebuilding our marriage."

The pros and cons of meeting the other woman

Let's start with the positives. You could get a better sense of proportion about their relationship. You could find out more information about their contact (when, where, how often). However, this can be a double-edged sword because it may be extremely painful—and there are gentler ways of uncovering this material. Similarly, it will provide her with a more balanced picture of you and your relationship and she might also find out some uncomfortable material, for example, that you're still having sex or have been reading her texts. Finally, confronting the other woman could help you to feel less powerless. Having said that, you could also be falling into the "something must be done" trap; contacting the mistress is certainly "something." However, often it is better to do nothing and to let a better "something" emerge over the coming months.

Let's look in detail at the downsides of contacting her. My main concern is magical thinking. For example: "Perhaps if she sees how much I love him, or I remind her of all the children involved, she will think again and get her talons out of him." In addition, the meeting could easily descend into you threatening her or getting angry and aggressive. This can encourage retaliation, at a later date, or her painting you as the guilty party, for upsetting her, and herself as innocent. She could also drip all sorts of poison into your heart; after all, she is not the most impartial witness about your husband and his feelings! Finally, remember, every word and gesture of this meeting will be reported (and probably distorted) to your husband. How will it play out to him? Could it seem like further proof that you're manipulative or controlling or that your marriage is beyond saving?

If you decide to confront her

There is no right or wrong decision, since each situation is different and you're the expert on how you will behave. However, if you do decide to go ahead, I would make the following provisos:

- Don't go on the spur of the moment. You will be angry, frightened, or upset and this will not promote clear thinking. (I had one client who drove to her rival's house, after a few drinks for courage, then the other woman phoned the police and my client ended up in court for drunk driving.)

- Think about what you want to achieve.

- Double-check that it is realistic.

- Make the meeting time limited. You are not two friends meeting for coffee.

- Be calm and listen to her. (Don't jump in even if she says something monstrous; bite your cheek instead.)

- Walk away if you feel you're likely to explode.

- Once again, remember it will all be repeated to your husband.

How to combat the other woman

She is filling your husband's head with negative thoughts and half-truths and stopping him from giving your marriage another chance. So how do you neutralize her influence and take back the initiative?

"I discovered that my husband's 'friendship' was a fully blown physical affair for seven years, starting when I was pregnant with our first child, with a couple of breaks in that time. The other woman started stalking me online when my husband didn't leave, also repeatedly phoning me, and staying silent on the phone late at night.

My husband said some terrible things and always talked about the love of his life (not me) and so on. However, I just refused to rise to it (most of the time) and gave him a firm ultimatum for making up his mind, telling him I was willing to try, but only if he stopped seeing her altogether and we went to counseling; then secretly crying to exhaustion when he went to work.

We had a couple of false starts when he lied about seeing her (even to the counselor), but finally, five years ago during a last-ditch vacation, he finally admitted everything that had happened (because I had found out everything when I discovered a secret email account!) and he committed to his family and trying to work it out with me.

I would say it took about six months for the veil to completely lift for him, helped of course by her actions against me, which showed him that perhaps she wasn't the person he thought; although in fact I bear her no malice really as he treated her shockingly too. I feel very sorry for her actually; she may have damaged me enormously, but in fact she damaged herself far more ..."

Don't try to control her

If you can't control your husband, you certainly can't control his "friend" or partner in his affair! However, it is tempting to expect your husband to work a miracle, by for example telling her not to call the house or stopping her dropping by at his office; then getting upset when he fails or, worse still, accusing him of encouraging her. If you are officially separated and he's already seeing another woman, it is equally common to try to disrupt her social life, or make things difficult, by changing access visits at the last minute or trying to stipulate what your children can or cannot do.

What's the alternative? Although you can't control her, what she says or what she does; you can control your response to her—at least in front of your husband. For example, you could rise above her petty ways or resist the invitation to make sarcastic comments about her.

So how do you do that? Take a couple of deep breaths and then a couple more. However sorely tempted, wait 24 hours before firing off a text (to the other woman or your husband) and any other behavior designed to resolve the situation (or make you feel better). The next day, if it's still a good idea by all means go ahead. My suspicion is that you will have forgotten all about it.

Don't run her down

You might want to open your husband's eyes and reveal just what a "nasty piece of work" she really is. However, let's be honest, you are hardly neutral and he will either discount everything you say or jump to her defense. If you know the other woman well, because she was one of your friends, it is doubly tempting to point out all her failings—and have the rest of your friendship circle bad-mouth or ostracize her. Unfortunately, if it seems that the "whole world" is against her, your husband could feel obliged to ride to her rescue, believe she really needs him (unlike you, whom everybody is supporting), or feel unable to abandon her (when she is so hurt).

What's the alternative? Although you can't point out her faults, you can encourage your husband to think about the impact of her behavior. The best way to achieve this goal is to ask questions. For example: "How do you think our daughter felt when she marched up while you were collecting her from school?" or "What will her children think about you?" Remember, questions start with who, what, why, when, and how. They don't invite yes or no answers, for example: "Don't you think she's taken leave of her senses?" If there are a million and one things that you're burning to say, start a private diary, but please, please don't tell your husband—or her! If she's an ex-friend, you can't control your other friends' behavior, but you can tell them that there's no need to punish her on your behalf.

Don't play games

By this I mean indulging in psychological warfare, such as phoning her cell phone and hanging up or sitting outside her place of work; making outright threats, particularly of a criminal nature such as damaging her property; or turning into a trickster, for example "borrowing: your husband's cell phone and sending texts while posing as him. This is especially important if she is using such tactics herself.

What's the alternative? You're going to play the reasonable, loving wife while she plays the deranged, wronged woman. If she does become abusive, start a log of her calls and note down anything that could be construed as stalking or harassment, (with dates, times, and basic details). Although this behavior is upsetting and worrying, try to reframe it as proof of her true nature (which could be presented to your husband). If she is truly frightening or your children are at risk, don't hesitate to contact the police and take legal advice.

Keep your powder dry

By this point, you've probably realized this is not going to be resolved overnight and you are going to have to play the long game. Therefore, you should use my strategies for neutralizing her sparingly. For example, do not report every strange call and, instead, wait until you have a body of compelling evidence. I would ask questions that invite your husband to consider her behavior and character only on an occasional basis—overuse can dull the effectiveness. It is especially important to hold any dynamite strategies in reserve—for example threatening to tell her husband—because you never know when you might need them.

What's the alternative? Running around, getting increasingly agitated, and shooting yourself in the foot. The other risk is of unexpected outcomes, such as telling her husband who then throws her out so that she becomes even more needy toward your partner.

A positive note

It has been hard to step into the shoes of the other woman, in order to understand her better and therefore counteract her more effectively, and to look at the similarities between your reactions. So I want to give you some hope—and a reminder of what you are aiming to achieve—by concluding with the rest of the letter we saw earlier (see page 171):

"... He is now a different husband. In fact it saddens me that we had the relationship we did for so many years. I buried my head in the sand; I didn't see his unhappiness; I didn't see the awful way he was treating me, I was too wrapped up in the children.

Things are good now though. We have had another baby; we have a lovely family; my husband is very happy and loving toward me; he finally feels he can talk to me. In a way, I think the fact that I stayed has given him some confidence, so that he's no longer worried about talking to me about difficult subjects."

Love Coach's Three Key Things to Remember

- The other woman must be in a dark place if she thinks another woman's husband is going to turn her life around.

- You cannot control the other woman, but you can control your reaction to her.

- If your husband is really trying to choose between you and the other woman, be the better person and someone with whom he'd want to spend the rest of his life.

CHAPTER TEN

How can I keep sane in an insane situation?

"I received a text message to another woman that wasn't intended for me. Subsequently, my husband admitted to having an emotional affair with a coworker and that he no longer wanted to be with me, because he didn't want to 'miss his chance' with this other woman.

Since my discovery, she has gone into therapy; decided that, yes, things have to end with them (because she needs to get her stuff together and also to respect both her and our marriages); and has minimized contact as much as possible. He says he has always had doubts, really serious doubts, and that it was a mistake to marry me. At the same time, he tells me how great and caring and wonderful I am.

He has decided to stay (for now) and 'work on it.' He does tell me that he cares about me, loves me, and that nothing I am going to do is going to push him away or make him leave me right now. He will be there for me and he wants to figure it out, too. However, it still feels that he's just doing this to appease me and there's not a lot of hope. How do I manage this feeling and get outside of my own head?'

Time and time again, I have stressed the importance of keeping calm. In that way, you can listen to your husband, judge the real seriousness of the situation, and negotiate with him—rather than order him about, beg for change, or appease and hope for the best. If you stay calm, you can also keep a sense of proportion about the other woman, because a lot of her power to ruin your life is in your own head. However, I know this is a tough ask—especially at moments when everything feels hopeless, you're completely overwhelmed with panic, so angry that you lash out or every fiber of your body is saying "run, run, run." Fortunately, I have some tools that will help you to cope and stay with my program—even if everything seems designed to make you lose your cool.

Six strategies for keeping calm

At first glance, these strategies do not look particularly powerful. However, in combination, they will not only transform this situation but also make every corner of your life better.

Take things one day at a time

I often say to my clients, "I know things are hard at the moment and that you think you're losing your mind, but can you cope with the situation today?" Most of them look at me rather incredulously. Of course they can. It's when they imagine everything stretching into the future for months and months, and maybe even years. And that's my point. If you stay fixed on now, today and possibly no farther ahead than the weekend, you are probably going to be all right.

Why it is so difficult: Our minds are constantly wandering off into both the past and the future. Either kicking ourselves, for example, that we did not set off earlier, and therefore get stuck in traffic, or worrying ahead about what will happen when we finally reach our destination—even though there are often no real consequences to being late and we're not actually missing that much. In the meantime, we can't enjoy the moment, listening to the radio, or watching the trees being tossed by the wind, because we're not actually in the present. Even when we're not particularly stressed, we have trained our minds to look forward. For example, nobody enjoys washing the dishes, so we tell ourselves we can have a sit down and a cup of coffee in a moment. Except that, when we finish, we can't relax and enjoy the break because we're already mentally going through a list of what we "must" do next.

Turn it around: A couple of times a day, bring your attention onto what you're doing right now—even if it is a dull or monotonous task. If washing the dishes, take pleasure in the warmth of the water or the way the detergent makes the grease float off the plate. Alternatively, you could enjoy the miracle of your body. How your fingers respond to your thoughts and move accordingly. Take a deep breath or two and register the air going in and out through your nostrils. If your mind starts to worry about an unknowable future, remind yourself: "one day at a time."

Accept your feelings

I spend a remarkably large amount of my counseling in reassuring my clients that it's all right to have whatever feeling they are experiencing. For example, it's normal to feel a deep sadness if your husband says, "You were the love of his life," (but are not any longer) or to be full of rage when he promises one thing, but does another. My clients reply that they don't like sadness and anger. Of course, they have my complete sympathy; these are uncomfortable feelings. However, the other options are not that attractive either, for example, being only half a human, by rationalizing the feelings away, or burying them by working too hard, with alcohol, comfort eating, or medication from the doctor (which is fine on a temporary basis, if the pain becomes too much, but is no formula for the long term).

Why it is so difficult: When we're young, our brains are not mature enough to deal with painful or difficult emotions by ourselves and we need our parents to pick us up, cradle us in their arms, and soothe us. Unfortunately, many parents are uncomfortable themselves with sadness, anger, or tears. Instead of holding us until we've calmed down, they will send us to our rooms, tease us, bribe us with candies, or tell us, "Don't make me mad." So we learn that if we want to be acceptable, and therefore loved, we shouldn't have these feelings. It is even tougher for small boys who are told that big boys don't cry. (For more on what we need as babies and small children, and the impact of not getting it, read my book *I Love You But You Always Put Me Last*.)

Turn it around: Instead of living on autopilot and largely ignoring your feelings until they become so strong that they swamp you, I'd like you to start to name them to yourself. For example: "I am feeling annoyed." Just identifying them will take them down by a couple of degrees and make them more manageable. It is also helpful to know that it isn't, for example, anger or rage or even fury. At this point, I don't want you to do anything more than to accept and witness the feeling.

If you have started to live in the moment, ask yourself, "Can I cope with feeling annoyed right now?" In most cases, the answer is "Yes," but if it's "No," take a couple of deep breaths; in a moment, I will discuss some other options.

I often ask clients to keep a feelings diary, in which they jot down how their feelings change throughout the day; I would strongly recommend that you start one too. Firstly, a diary will help you honor and therefore accept your feelings. Secondly, you will realize that no feeling lasts forever. The distress is soon replaced by something else; maybe it builds to anger or perhaps it dissipates to resignation, but you're not stuck feeling upset to the same degree for the whole day. However if you try to push away the distress, rather than to accept and witness it, the feeling will gather power and ambush you.

Challenge your thoughts

When you begin to notice and name your feelings, you will see that they often come accompanied by thoughts. Most probably, you will have lots and lots of them and they will be full of black and white language, for example "I will *never* ever recover," or "She will *always* pop up when things are going well between us."

Why it is so difficult: Sometimes clients mistake thoughts for emotions; for example, "I feel the other woman is going to steal my husband" is a thought. The feeling might be "threatened" or "anxious" or maybe even "relief," because that's better than him coming and going. When you notice your thoughts—and separate them from your feelings—you will begin to see how much your interpretation of an event affects your reaction. So if you think the other woman is going to shift from phoning and hanging up to turning up on your doorstep, you will probably feel frightened, but if you think that she's sad and deluded, your feeling is more likely to be one of pity.

Turn it around: Instead of letting your thoughts go around and around in your head, write them all down. Don't censor yourself, just take dictation. Once they are all down, look at the exaggerations and challenge their validity. For example, where is the proof that you will *never*, ever recover—even when you're seventy? A more honest answer would be: "It will take me a long time to recover"; still upsetting, but nowhere near as bleak.

Sometimes it helps to turn statements into questions. For example: "I will never get this woman out of my hair" makes you feel helpless, whereas "How do I get this woman out of my hair?" would encourage you to read the relevant chapter of my book again. Sometimes, your thoughts will chain two unrelated parts of your life together; for example, "I'm having trouble with my boss and my husband and that proves I'm hopeless with men." However, in reality, three quarters of the women in your office find your boss difficult and he's a totally different character from your husband.

If you're feeling overwhelmed at any point, remember my mantra: *Accept the feelings* and *challenge the thoughts*.

Learn to self-soothe

Even after you have accepted your feeling, named it (and therefore witnessed it), challenged any accompanying thoughts, and taken a few deep breaths, you might still be overwhelmed. Don't worry, I have another tool up my sleeve. What do I mean by self-soothing? In a nutshell, this is anything that helps you to live with the feeling, rather than blank it out. (See also "Six unhelpful coping strategies to avoid" later in this chapter.) This could involve looking after yourself, by for example having a hot bath rather than telling yourself that you must clean the kitchen floor, or being kind to yourself, for instance by telling yourself, "I'm doing really well under really difficult circumstances." You could phone up a supporter and unload your distress or read one of my books and turn the setback into a learning opportunity.

Why it is so difficult: It is very tempting to expect your husband to soothe you; after all, that's what love is all about—and you're right, but only up to a point. Worse still, you may get angry with him for not doing it: "You've caused all this pain, so making me feel better is the least that you can do!" Therefore, you're upset about his original crime of infidelity and a second one of not clearing it up effectively. Yet you are asking somebody to soothe you who's not good at soothing himself; otherwise, he wouldn't have got into this mess in the first place.

Turn it around: I know it's tough, but you've got to take responsibility for your own life, instead of outsourcing it, and therefore learn to soothe yourself. So where does this fit in with loving someone and wanting to help them? As I have explained, your partner is your companion on your journey through life. You can ask him for help over a fence or to ford a river, but you can't expect him to carry you, and vice versa.

Choose how to react

Once you can remain calm even when stressed and upset, you will be able to stop, think through your response and only then act or speak. In effect, you will be choosing your response, rather than reacting in the same old way—which is what got you into this mess—or just being on autopilot—not even clocking your behavior or noticing its impact.

Why it is difficult: It is much easier to blame, rather than to take responsibility for our reactions. For example: "He was right in my face, so I pulled his hair," or "I was tired and I'd had a couple of drinks, so I fired off a couple of emails telling her exactly what I thought." It might seem as if you have no choice but, in truth, you're not a prisoner of your feelings. You have a range of options, such as walking away from your angry partner or pouring the glass of wine back into the bottle and having an early night.

Another problem is that some people think their feelings are "instructions" on how to behave. So, if you're angry, you should let it rip. Obviously, I don't want you to ignore your feelings but, instead, to consider them as "clues" about how to react.

Turn it around: A wise decision requires you to take into consideration both heart and head. Accepting your feelings does not mean acting on each and every one. After all, your upset might be fleeting—and, when you examine your thoughts, it could be that you're more angry with yourself than your husband. However, if you're finding the same emotions coming around time and time again, it could be a *clue* that you need to act differently; for example, you have been too understanding or too flexible and need to put your foot down. However, when you are calm and choose how to react, you can report your feelings ("I can't go on like this for much longer because it feels like torture") or ask for what you really need ("Can I have a hug?"), rather than hoping he will guess. In most cases, there are several ways to be true to your feelings without creating more problems for yourself.

Look for the point of no return

I hope that you are beginning to see that you can work with your feelings rather being besieged by them. If you have been following the other five strategies and accepted your feelings (rather than categorizing them as good or bad), challenged your thoughts (and looked at the bigger picture), and self-soothed (rather than castigated yourself), you should be able to choose to be still, calm, and resilient, rather than blinded by emotion. However, if you have a tendency to flee or fight, it is important to look for the point of no return, at which you change from being reasonably calm, and still in control, into unhelpful or even harmful behavior. In this way, you have will have a backup plan if a new discovery or events become too much.

> *Why it is difficult: If you have been trained to ignore your feelings, and therefore discount them, or to become preoccupied by them, and therefore exaggerate and dramatize them to get noticed, it takes time to find a balance. So please don't give up or punish yourself. There will be setbacks; it is how you deal with them that counts.*

Turn it around: Be aware of where the feelings are in your body. Does your chest feel tight? Is there a lump in your throat? Do you fingers start to itch? Are you gritting your teeth? Does your stomach have a sinking feeling? Does your breathing become shallower and faster?

Next, be aware of the moment the feelings threaten to turn from tolerable to unmanageable. Before you reach the point of "I need a break. We can talk about this later when I'm calmer and can think straight." Then walk away.

It might take a while to understand your feelings and sometimes you will go past your point of no return, but please look at it as a learning opportunity and, next time, leave at an earlier stage.

Six unhelpful coping strategies to avoid

By now, you will have a good idea about what I'm going to discuss since I've touched on many of these issues before. However, the line between self-soothing (facing the problems, but taking the edge off the pain) and self-medicating (burying the pain and doing your best to forget your problems) can easily become blurred. Therefore, I think it is helpful to spell out what falls on the wrong side of the line.

Alcohol

The majority of women drink for stress reduction and relaxation. However, time and time again, I find my clients have undermined their good work by late-night drinking and dialing. Many women should have a notice pinned to their computers and smartphones: "Not to be operated under the influence of alcohol." If you are concerned about the amount you're consuming, keep a strict internal log. The generally agreed recommendation is for no more than two drinks on any night and none at all on a few nights a week.

According to the Centers for Disease Control and Prevention they estimated that nearly 14 million women in the US binge drink about three times a month a. If you're concerned, do the CAGE test:

C Have you ever felt that you should CUT down your drinking?

A Have people ANNOYED you by criticizing your drinking?

G Have you ever felt GUILTY about your drinking?

E Have you had an EYE-OPENER? For example, have you ever
   had a drink first thing in the morning to steady your nerves or
   to get rid of a hangover? Have you fallen asleep on the train
   or bus and woken up at the end of the line? Have you had
   blackouts where you have woken up somewhere unexpected
   or someone has had to rescue you from a dangerous situation?

If you answer "yes" to two questions, you could have a drinking
problem. If you answer "yes" to three or more, you definitely
have a drinking problem.

What's the alternative? Eat something before you go home from
work, so you don't walk in the door tired and with blood sugar
levels so low that you're craving alcohol. Look at other ways to
handle stress. I've already explained how becoming assertive can
prevent you from feeling unheard, powerless, and frustrated—
and needing to medicate away the pain. In addition, plan activities to relieve stress early in the evening when you might be
tempted to have a drink, such as doing yoga, going for a run,
putting on a relaxation tape, or taking a trip to the movies or
theater.

Comfort eating

We eat for a wide variety of reasons beyond nourishing our body:
for example, to reduce stress, relieve anxiety, or boredom and to
feel less lonely. Carbohydrates and sugary foods, in particular, fill
us up and make us feel better. However, comfort eating not only
leaves you feeling bloated and guilty, but also does nothing for
your self-esteem, which is probably at an all-time low. In the
worst cases, it can lead to another round of eating, in a desperate
attempt to quash those difficult feelings.

What's the alternative? Try mindful eating; in other words, being
aware of what you're eating rather than just shoveling it into
your mouth. Look at your plate and the textures, colors and
shapes. How does it smell? Eat slowly and think about the taste

and texture. A lot of processed foods are designed to be swallowed, rather than chewed, so that you eat more. Put your fork down between bites. How do you feel after eating? Does it agree with you? What about an hour or two after eating? Do you feel sluggish? How does your stomach feel?

My advice would be to cook as much as possible, rather than just reach for what is readily available—processed foods. If you're often short of time, make a big pot of soup or roast a chicken, so that there is cooked food available when you get home. In this way, you will be looking after yourself, rather than self-medicating.

Ranting

Whether face-to-face or by text and email, ranting occurs when you're not just tempted to say "and another thing …," but to do it over and over again. Instead of dealing with the problem or facing your emotions, you're just vomiting everything out—all over your partner.

What's the alternative? A lot of stress and misery in the world comes from being too attached to what we want. So stop and ask yourself "why was this so important to me?." Had I become so attached to a piece of magical thinking ("Going out would make him remember we were fun together") that, when it was disrupted (he was kept late at work), I erupted and started ranting? Alternatively, if it was truly important that I say something, what would be a better way to make my case?

Suppressing

As I've said before, when you're trying to save your marriage, it is easy to put your own needs to one side and focus on your partner's needs. The result is that your life becomes a catalog of resentments, slights, and injustices.

What's the alternative? You have two choices. Firstly, next time you're about to add to that pile, you could stop, be assertive, and speak to your partner. Secondly, you could be generous and decide to let him have his own way on this occasion, because ultimately it is not that big a deal. The alternative is holding onto your resentment, sometimes for years and years. As the old adage goes, "Resentment is like drinking a poison and waiting for the other person to die."

Overapologizing

I'm all in favor of an apology, if it is gladly given and genuinely felt. However, lots of times, the apologies are really saying, "I'm small and harmless; don't kick me." There is a slight variation in which you rescue your partner's thoughtless behavior by telling him not to worry about it or that it doesn't matter, when in reality it does.

What's the alternative? Instead of trying to escape from a difficult situation by apologizing, try being silent. Saying nothing is incredibly powerful—particularly on the phone—as people hate to leave a void. If you can sit with your discomfort for a moment, it is likely that your partner will say something instead, reveal more about his thinking, or perhaps even realize that he's in the wrong. Never underestimate the power of silence.

Acting out

> When small children or teenagers are unhappy, instead of saying something they slam doors, self-harm, pick on a smaller child at school, start shoplifting, and so on. When adults are unhappy and feel powerless, they can regress to similarly destructive behaviors.

What's the alternative? Delay the impulse to act. Notice your feelings, instead of trying to blank them out with action. Next, look at the losses and benefits of your proposed behavior. How do they weigh out, not just at this moment but in the medium and longer term? Finally, you are no longer a small child and therefore have more resources and options. What are the alternatives? Try making a list so you're aware of all the possibilities.

Five ways to be more alluring

I have covered how to cope on a day-to-day basis, so that you don't make matters worse and can buy time to start fixing the problems in your marriage. I have explained that much of the other woman's power is in your imagination. However, your husband is still infatuated and, even if he's fighting his desire to be with her, you're worried about the future.

"I discovered my husband was having an inappropriate friendship with an attractive, young work colleague (who happened to be newly married and pregnant!) Seeing the emails between them broke my heart and despite accepting on three separate occasions that the relationship had to stop to give our marriage a chance, the contact continued until recently, when I threatened to tell her husband (I just didn't know how else to stop it). The colleague is now on maternity leave, but I am terrified about what will happen when she returns to work.

We are really enjoying our time together now and he says he loves life with me and the children, but that he still sees me only as a friend and he needs passion in his life. At times, I see a spark, but this is only when he is comforting me when I cry or we are watching a romantic movie (and he's had a few glasses of wine). We had sex once a few months ago (at my instigation) and it was terrible, as he had his head turned away from me the whole time.

When I stroke his arms or face, he can be mean and say something like 'Don't do it for my benefit,' but other times he will snuggle up to me in bed. We briefly kiss on the lips, but this is always at my instigation. I am trying not to be pushy, but it's so hard to be ignored. I keep telling myself that it will take time (the last drama involving his colleague was only three weeks ago), as he says he gradually started shutting down to me years ago, but wonder if there is anything else I can do to help. I am mindful that the clock is ticking until his 'friend' returns to work."

What makes someone charismatic, influential, and the person everybody wants to be with? We imagine that it is beauty, being funny, or full of wisdom—all of which makes the task of winning back your beloved seem really daunting. However, I have been through all the research into leadership and discovered that personal magnetism is much simpler and something we can all achieve. What is particularly exciting is that many of these ideas replicate the experience of falling in love, and can be used to combat the appeal of the other woman.

Be completely present

The first way to be more alluring is really simple: being completely present in the moment and giving the other person our undivided attention. Cast your mind back to the beginning of your relationship: your beloved knew there was nowhere else you would rather be than with him, holding his hand or cuddling up to him. You'd tell him over and over again how much you loved him; you rearranged your plans to be with him; and if you went as far away as the next room you'd rush back to give him a quick kiss. No wonder he felt special, because he saw it reflected back in your eyes.

Unfortunately, once you're married, running a house, earning a living, and raising children, you seldom—if ever—give each other your undivided attention. You're too busy cooking meals, running a bath for the children, thinking about tomorrow's work meeting, or checking your Facebook page. Similarly your mind is racing down a "to-do" list and, at the moment, you're worrying about how each interaction will go, whether he's about to drop another bombshell, or how you might steer the conversation to gather more information about the other woman. So although you might be listening, and could perhaps repeat back what was said, it is registering in only half your brain, because the other half is churning away on other stuff.

Make it a reality: When your partner comes home, put down what you're doing and turn and face him. Even if you're washing the children in the bath, they are unlikely to drown in the few seconds that it takes to properly greet him. If feasible, put down any distractions and concentrate on the moment. In most cases, it won't matter if the meal is late because you've stopped chopping carrots and turned off the stove or if you finish your posting on Facebook later. If you get home after your partner, greet him *before* being sidetracked by demands from the children or feeding the cat as this gives a powerful message about your priorities.

By now I hope that you'll have started to follow my strategies for being calm and you're accepting your feelings, rather than trying to stigmatize them. However, if any disturbing thoughts pop into your head—and threaten to take your focus from being present with your husband—you can challenge them by telling yourself that you can think about it later. In that way, you will be living in the moment and completely present when you interact with your husband.

Finally, reinforce the fact that you're truly interested in what he's saying by nodding and smiling. You can also use the reflecting-back technique, where you repeat his last few words. For example: "So your boss lost his temper." In most cases, it will encourage him to open up further and tell you more about the story. Another technique, from the early stages of dating, is to ask lots of questions: "What did your colleagues think?" or "Did he stay angry for long?" When you're having a general conversation, try deepening it with a thought-provoking question; for example, "What made you happy when you were a child?" After all, to ask questions is to be hungry to get to know someone—or in this case rediscover them.

Be compassionate

It is easy to think, "Sure, he's stressed, unhappy, and pulled in two directions, but he's only got himself to blame." And you'd be right! However, there is a only a moment's pleasure in being right and it does long-term damage to your marriage. In effect, you're putting your husband in the wrong and making him feel bad about himself—and by extension, you too, for pulling him down. However, if you can be compassionate and accept him flaws and all, you're making an incredibly positive statement.

Babies arrive in the world and their parents think they are wonderful for simply being. However, before too long acceptance becomes conditional: "Eat your mashed rutabaga and smile at Granny." Guess what is the next time that we're perfect just the way we are? That's right, in the early stages of falling in love. Limerence not only makes you blind to your beloved's flaws (playing with his beard is cute rather than irritating), but also converts them into an asset ("It's great that he loves his mother so much because it shows that he respects women"), rather than having a more balanced or realistic attitude from years of living together ("It's fine that he loves his mother, but it means he rarely takes my side in any disagreement with her").

Make it a reality: Give him an empathy injection by identifying how he might be feeling and why. For example: "You must be feeling really guilty, because of all the upset," or "You're looking really tired, because you haven't been sleeping for the worry." If you don't quite identify his feeling, for example he feels shattered rather than tired, he will correct you. Ultimately, it doesn't matter if you get it 100 percent right, just that you've noticed and you care.

If you're finding it hard to be compassionate toward your husband, it is probably because you haven't extended the same kindness to yourself. So what generates self-compassion? Firstly, tell yourself that you're going through a hard time so are bound to make mistakes. Secondly, realize that your husband texting other women is a common enough experience—otherwise, I wouldn't have needed to write this book. How do you think those other women are coping? It's easy to think that everybody else is having it easier or doing better. However, they are probably managing in much the same way as you, with good days and bad ones. So don't punish yourself, but respond with understanding and forgive yourself.

Look for similarities

When we meet someone at a party or start a work project together, we're always looking for connections; for example, we were both born in the same place or like the music of Elton John. It reassures us that they are "people like us" and we will get on, or at least not be enemies. Obviously, this process goes into overdrive when we're falling in love and, even if you have no interest in each other's passions, such as sailing, you'll discover a burning desire to try them out.

In sharp contrast, settled couples are not involved in every corner of each other's lives. So if you think that sailing involves lots of ordering about, getting cold or wet, and seeing the same stretch of coastline over and over again, you'll join your partner only when the weather's good or he's planning a special journey. After all, you don't need to spend every minute together. Unfortunately, having space to follow separate interests can easily drift into separate lives and, worse still, no interest in each other's passions.

Make it a reality: We don't just bond over shared interests, but shared adversity too. So when your husband complains, for example, about feeling tired, don't say it serves him right, but look for similarities: "I haven't been sleeping properly either." Once you put your mind to it, you'll find that there are lots of matches. You're both worried about the future. Neither of you want to go back to "how things were"—because that's where the seeds for this pain were sown. You're both having trouble concentrating on anything for more than a few moments. Your moods are swinging between hopefulness and despair. I could go on, but I'll leave you to think about it. Every time you come up with a "Me too" moment—however bleak—it shows a connection and builds a bridge.

Obviously, it is helpful to have some positive similarities too. So show more of an interest in your partner's pastimes. For example, you could watch him compete in a sailing race or make up a picnic and help to pack up the boat for the winter. You could also look for new interests to pursue together.

If you're still in crisis mode, and he doesn't want to spend much, or any, quality time together, you can still add a positive note to a negative discussion by ending with something that you can agree on. For example: "We both want the best for our children."

Increase the positives

When researchers at the University of Washington in Seattle looked at what made some marriages succeed while others failed, they found it took five positive interactions (for example, smiles, compliments, thank yous) to cancel out a negative one (for example, a sour expression, criticism, righteous indignation). However, for a marriage to thrive rather than just tick over, I recommend aiming for twenty positives to each negative.

Make it a reality: When you're in crisis and worrying about the future of your relationship, it is easy to be defensive, critical, or angry with your partner and to take the good things for granted or, worse still, to be contemptuous about his efforts to make things better. Before too long, your whole relationship has been overwhelmed with negativity and who wants to live like that?

Don't worry, I'm not going to ask you to be a saint about his bad behavior. However, you can put positives into even the most negative arguments by validating your partner. For example, "You have a good point there"; "I can see where you're coming from"; or even something simple such as "I understand."

I'd also recommend keeping a "gratitude diary," in which you record everything positive (rather than taking them for granted) and, if it involves your husband, telling him rather than keeping it to yourself.

Finally, we tend to live up or down to the picture that people paint of us. So if you complain that your partner is selfish, he could think "I have to be," and harden his determination to get his own way. If you tell him "you're a bastard," he could think "I've got nothing to lose if I email my friend." Conversely, if you compliment your partner about some behavior, he'll probably start acting in that way. For example: "I've been impressed about how you think everything through," will encourage more thoughtfulness; "You've been really kind," will encourage more consideration.

Articulate a positive vision

The final way to be alluring won't come as a surprise, because I discussed it in "The importance of framing your story" (see page 103), but it's important so let's recap. Either your husband has woven an alternative future around this other woman or she's articulating the vision herself; either way it promises eternal love, plentiful sex, and a happy ending. Meanwhile, you're left peddling reality: distraught kids, broken home, and financial ruin. It's not difficult to see why your message is falling on deaf ears. Of course, you can scare people with pessimism, but optimism is always going to be more popular.

Make it a reality: Look back through this book and make a note of everything you've learned about yourself and your marriage. Next, think about everything you'd like to change. Aim for practical goals rather than vague ambitions. What progress have you made already? What benefits have you seen? What more would you like to do? Write your findings down—to make it more real. Finally, ask yourself how you could turn this into a positive vision of the future that you could articulate to your husband.

If your husband is totally closed off to any talk about a future together, you can still tell him about the changes you're making to yourself and ask for any feedback. Has he noticed any changes? What has been the impact on him? This discussion will show that you're committed to behaving differently and offer the potential of a different and better relationship.

Love Coach's Three Key Things to Remember

- Men find it difficult to communicate in highly charged situations when they feel threatened or vulnerable.

- Accept your feelings, because they are a natural response to a difficult situation, but challenge your thoughts because they could exaggerate the threat and turn a set back into a catastrophe.

- You can't match the excitement of a new relationship, but you can duplicate some of the behaviors and begin to rebuild your loving connection with your husband.

CHAPTER ELEVEN

How do I know when it is best to give up and stop trying?

"One month ago, I discovered that my partner of ten years has been having an affair over the internet for the past eight months. I moved out straightaway, but we work together and so still see each other every day. I thought he would apologize and try to get me back, but he hasn't. He says that he still loves me, but is not sure what he wants. He knows that he can't be with this other woman, but says that she is his best friend.

He is still emailing her, telling her that he loves her. I am trying so hard to be strong, trying to put what you say into practice and not pressure him, but finding it so hard. We have socialized a fair amount in the month since we've split, and he has commented about how nice it has been to spend time as friends together— but he is still not convinced he wants to be with me.

He is contacting her; he is planning weekends away with friends and not telling me. He is ignoring me when I ask him direct questions about his plans for weekends and so on. It hurts so much every time he blocks me and I fear that I'm losing the motivation to fight.

I feel like he's trying to just hurt me until I give up. The longer we're apart, the more I realize that he doesn't care for me and I don't know if he ever will again. When do I give up and move on?"

Although you don't really want to end your marriage, you're frightened of wasting even more time and emotional energy on a relationship that could be going nowhere. It feels like you're hitting your head against a brick wall, so perhaps you should bow to the inevitable? Except the minute that you consider the reality of life without your husband, you're swept away by a wave of despair. So you swing back to soldiering on, but the pain is so great you don't think that this is a viable option either. If this dilemma sounds familiar, how do you cut through the confusion and make a decision one way or the other?

Five questions to help you find clarity

People who get stuck in the "Should I give up or fight on?" trap are looking at judging their relationship like a judge in rather black or white terms of "guilty or not guilty" or, more accurately, "over or not?" However, in my experience, it is better to be like a doctor and make a diagnosis: "How healthy is this relationship and can it still be saved?" So here are five questions to help you do just that.

Am I just temporarily feeling down?

It could be that this is the worst time to decide if your relationship has a future. Perhaps you're tired, when everything seems worse; have been letting yourself go, because if your husband doesn't love you, you don't love yourself enough to look after yourself; stressed because of extra pressure at work when previously you'd have been able to cope with his love and support; or it's a significant vacation or anniversary, when you remember all the good times and worry about the future. If you think this may be a temporary down, don't ignore it. Remember, my mantra: Accept your feelings. Perhaps you need extra help: speak to your doctor, find more supporters, or maybe take a short break away.

If, however, this "down" is part of a pattern, it could be that your relationship has gone past the point of no return. For example: you talk yourself up, and then crash, or concentrate all your energy on one particular rescue strategy and, when it fails, are faced with the full scale of the problem. However, don't jump to any conclusion until you have looked at the rest of the questions.

Am I oversimplifying the situation?

When we examine our own motivations, we come up with a multitude of interlocking reasons for our behavior—some positive, some defensive, and some in-between. When we examine our own feelings, there is a complex set of competing emotions.

At the moment, you may probably alternate between hope and despair, joy and misery, anger, and love. If someone asked you how you have been feeling, it would take about fifteen minutes to explain and also would depend on which moment in the last few days they are asking about. However, while we are ready to accept our own complexity, we tend to put our partner's motivations down to only *one* thing: "He doesn't love me" or "He wants to hurt me." To top it all, it can tip over into thinking that you know your husband's feelings and therefore can simply *assume* what is going on in his head: for example "This means he's moving on," or "He doesn't care about me." If you're not careful, your assumption—built on smoke and mirrors—becomes your solid reality and you have talked yourself into giving up.

Next time, you find yourself coming up with one overriding explanation for your husband's behavior or assuming that you can mind read, tell yourself, "This is the age of uncertainty. I might hate not knowing, but it is worse to guess and guess wrong. So let it drop for now." Remember, although you're going to accept your feelings, you're going to challenge your thoughts.

If, however, you keep saying "Yes, but ..." when you try to disengage your overactive mind, it could be that you truly have had enough and need to review whether you have the energy to continue. The next three questions will help you to decide if this is the case.

Am I still growing?

It is your worst nightmare: "What if I put all this effort into saving my marriage and he throws it all back in my face?" Certainly, I wouldn't want you to endure all this pain and soul-searching for nothing. However, this program is not just about saving your marriage but also about learning about yourself and improving communication. Obviously, the best outcome is that your husband falls back in love and you both live happily ever after. However, there are other outcomes worth having. If your marriage can't be saved, but you and your husband learn to become better coparents, it is worth pressing on, at least for now. Finally, if you are finding a more realistic view of love, trying not to make the same mistakes again, and developing some self-compassion, I think you will emerge a stronger person and go onto find lasting love with someone else.

So if you're still learning, improving communication, listening to your partner and yourself, I think it is worth continuing the fight. The relationship is either healthy or you will find a healthy outcome, so press on.

If, however, you have already found a sort of peace between you and your husband—and you can cooperate over matters to do with the children—or have taken all the lessons from this dismal situation possible, then maybe you have your answer.

Have I really tried everything?

It might seem that you've explored all the possibilities, but most people have simply used the same failed strategy over and over again—just bigger and bigger. For example: shouting louder or sulking for longer. So if there are still other strategies to try—and this book is full of them—it is worth fighting on. Even if your marriage is beyond saving, you will be able to tell yourself that "I did all I could," and that will help you to feel less guilty and to make a better recovery.

If, however, you have read this book, reread it, tried all the strategies, and still keeping coming up against a brick wall, you have another damning answer. But before you make up your mind, there is one final question—perhaps the most important one—to ask and three final strategies to try.

Do I have enough love to give without getting anything back—at least in the short term?

This fifth question is the key one. If you still love your husband enough to be compassionate about his feelings and can be generous enough to keep giving without getting anything back, for a little bit longer, there is still hope that your marriage can be saved.

If all you can think is "after what he's done ...," "after what he's said ...," or "yes, but he's got to ...," then either it's too soon after a nasty discovery, and you're still in shock, or your marriage is truly over.

Reviewing your answers

I hope that my five questions will have given you a lot to think about. If you're still uncertain, imagine that your heart is like a cupboard. If you open the door and there is something left to feed your relationship, that's a good sign. If the cupboard is empty or it feels like you would have to cut off a pound of your own flesh, that's a bad sign. However, I'd like to think that the fact that you've bought this book means that you still have enough love left—and that means it's not too late.

Three final strategies

By this point, you should have a better understanding of why your husband was drawn to the other woman, why he's finding it so hard to give her up, and her part in the problem. I've also explained how your distress depends on how you interpret events, as well as given advice on how to stay calm, negotiate rather than order a way forward, and to become more alluring. But what happens if the situation is still impossible and intolerable?

"I've learned a lot about our 22-year marriage from your books. Our arguing style was dysfunctional and we both had stopped having relaxation time together, and instead spent every weekend working on our different projects.

After a 26-year-old intern spent a month working with my husband, he started sending long, intimate emails to her, even when he wouldn't talk to me, and began an emotional affair. Last year, they started meeting up, sometimes in secret (my husband inventing meetings to be with her). His excuse, when confronted, was that she was 'just a friend' (one he says inappropriate things to), but my excessive reactions meant that he 'had' to keep it secret. Recently he has admitted that he has a crush on this young lady, but refuses to stop his inappropriate friendship with her.

After two years of ups and downs, I alternate between calm conversations, crying, and sometimes shouting. I know that when I am calm, our communication is better, but sometimes I'm over-whelmed by everything, and react emotionally, which he can't take. He wanted to continue in the same way, with his semi-

commitment to me, and keep his special friend, but I asked him to choose. But when I do this he says that she is not our only problem (of course!), and that I will never trust him again, any way. This seems to be an excuse not to change anything. So I've told him I want a temporary separation.

At the moment he's in the spare room, but as soon as we've arranged other accommodation, he'll go there. He says he doesn't want to, and feels sad, but is adamant that he won't give up his friend, whom he says he needs, and who makes him feel happy. I know this is a fantasy relationship, so does he.

I feel that he is behaving egocentrically, but he still says I'm overreacting to his 'friendship.' Our teenage children are also very upset, and want us to solve the problem (so do I!), but we seem to be at a stalemate. What else can I do?"

Have time off

You've been working around the clock to save your marriage: reading books, having counseling, turning yourself inside out. In the meantime, your husband has done nothing productive—and by continuing to text the other woman, doing plenty that is destructive. No wonder you are exhausted, demoralized, and full of resentment. Time and time again, I find people in your situation will see only two ways forward: Fix (find another magic solution) or Flee (ask for a divorce). However, there is a third option: Time off or what Buddhists would call "nondoing."

As you've probably realized by now, turning around your marriage is more of a marathon than a sprint. Therefore, there's nothing wrong with having a break to rest, replenish your energy supplies, look after yourself, and take a vacation from worrying about the future.

Turn it into a reality: Think about what you'd like to do, not what would help your marriage. For example, if you'd like a vacation with your girlfriends—book it. Of course, time away will give him and the other woman space to be together, but has patroling their contact changed anything—beyond exhausting you? If you're a mother, what you need for yourself will probably be last on your list of priorities, but imagine that you have permission to put yourself first—if only for a few months. What would you do? How could you pamper yourself? What would happen if you just went with the flow for a while?

Radical acceptance

In many ways, this concept goes hand in hand with the last one. Instead of struggling to change the situation, you have to accept where you are right now: your husband doesn't love you and he's involved with someone else. I call it radical acceptance because I'd like you to accept it deep down—acceptance is actually the only way out of this hellhole.

I can see you looking open-mouthed; you can't quite process what I'm saying and part of you thinks that I'm suggesting throwing in the towel. No, that's not what I'm saying, not at all. Unfortunately, there are lots of myths about acceptance that make it harder to reach—let alone achieve radical acceptance; also, popular culture celebrates never giving up. No wonder we imagine that if we don't accept something and simply refuse to put up with it, it will somehow magically change—almost as if willpower alone will change everything. So let's look at these myths and fears about acceptance:

- *Acceptance equals approval.* With this myth, we believe that if we accept something, we can't change it. However, the reverse is true. Unless we accept reality, we can't begin to make the situation better. For example, I was stranded by a budget airline—late at night—in a foreign city with just a sheet of paper to tell me what to do and no staff to advise. I could have railed against the airport clerk who'd shown us where to collect our bags about the incompetence and unfairness of abandoning us. I could have wished that I'd flown with a larger, better-staffed and more responsible airline. I could have tried to find a telephone number for the company back in the US and told them to "sort it out." However, the airport was about to shut down and I'd be better off finding a hotel, something to eat, and booking an alternative flight for the morning. I certainly did not approve of the treatment I'd received, but I had to accept where I was and set about making my situation as bearable as possible.

- *Acceptance means being passive or simply giving up.* I think acceptance is a longer game than this myth suggests. At the airport, I had accepted that there was nothing I could do late at night in a strange airport. However, when I got home, eighteen hours later than expected, I researched my rights, wrote to the airline concerned, and several weeks later received a refund and compensation.

- *Acceptance is a feeling.* I think this is perhaps the most pernicious myth about acceptance, because we are left waiting to feel better. However, acceptance is a choice too, and therefore not just an emotion. Often it's something we have to do over and over again, because sometimes acceptance will last only a few hours or need to be repeated on a regular basis. However, we can choose to accept the situation—or conversely that something has gone on for long enough and it's time for action.

Turn it into a reality: Instead of trying to change your husband's feelings, the behavior of the other woman, or make an unfair world more caring, you could accept what is and respond in the most appropriate way possible. In effect, you are showing willingness to engage with reality, rather than willfulness—trying to impose your will on reality. Ask yourself what you can do in this situation. Start with small irritations that are not connected to your husband: for example, a long queue to buy tickets at a train station—what is the reality and what can you do about it? You could go straight to the front of the queue, but probably be turned away; or sigh and keep looking at your watch, but what would that change?; or you could accept that there are five people in front of you and either try a ticket machine or wait your turn. Which option is going to be the least stressful and most effective? Once you've begun to practice radical acceptance in minor scenarios, you can move onto apply it to your relationship crisis.

Withdrawing

If radical acceptance is a difficult strategy to take on board, the final one is even harder. However, I'm not suggesting giving up, but a tactical withdrawal. When my first puppy refused to come back when in the local park, I would call his name, "Flash," over and over again and then go over to fetch him, in case he got into danger or annoyed someone. However, my dog-training instructor explained that I was just teaching Flash to ignore me. He didn't need to listen or prioritize me over his own interests, because I would always wait for him. Are you beginning to see the parallels? My instructor suggested running in the opposite direction or, if Flash still didn't come, to hide behind a tree; in this way, I could use his natural puppy's separation anxiety to encourage him to watch me. Guess what? Flash had great recall.

My second puppy, Pumpkin, is a gun dog; so I had a different trainer and he added a second element—which could also help with your husband! He recommended that if Pumpkin was not paying sufficient attention I should start doing something really interesting. So if Pumpkin was off sniffing the hedgerows, I would drop a cookie in the long grass by my feet and call him over to find it. In this way, I became a source of good times to my puppy. In your predicament, you are probably being really predictable and, if you're staying at home gnashing your teeth and wailing, not very interesting.

Turn it into a reality: Instead of putting your life on hold until the crisis is over, get out of the house and find out what life has to offer. This could be dating again—after all, what's sauce for goose is sauce for the gander. However, please don't force yourself to see other men. I want you to be genuine and truthful, rather than issuing threats or game-playing. There are lots of other options: joining a choir or the National Parent Teacher Association of your children's school, taking an evening class, or even going skydiving. The choice, obviously, depends on your interests. You might spark your husband's interest and it's certainly better than another night at home tracking his computer browsing history or reading her Facebook page.

If you cannot cope with your husband's continued contact with the other woman, please ask him to leave and discuss a temporary separation. I know he may go straight around to the other woman's house, but it might not be the blissful union that you fear. There is a big difference between typing sweet nothings and turning them into reality. What's more, when he's standing on her doorstep with a huge suitcase, he might not be quite so appealing. Even if she does welcome him with open arms, their relationship will be tested in the real world and most probably be found wanting. Meanwhile, you will protect your love for him by withdrawing before he destroys any remaining feelings of good-will, compassion, or patience.

Negotiating a temporary separation

I know a temporary separation is going to seem like failing, but I'd like you to reframe the situation. Here is another opportunity to improve your communication—especially if you take your time to discuss all the implications, rather than just demand one or use it as a threat. Although this might feel like your darkest moment, it could also be the beginning of your fight back. If you handle it well, your husband could come away thinking, "She really listened to me," or "She didn't get angry or tearful, so per-haps things can change." Here are a few topics to discuss.

- *How long?* At this point, you will probably have no idea how long a separation would be helpful—especially if you're both exhausted and in need of a cooling-off period. However, it helps if your temporary separation is not open-ended. So ask for a review to be built in after two, three, or six months. You can always extend the temporary separation if it turns out to be not enough.

- *What contact will you have?* Will you see each other at social sit-uations, such as friends' parties? Perhaps you need a complete break for a while? Alternatively, you could meet for coffee and exchange mail. If you do, will you talk about "us" or keep it chatty and light? What about access to the kids? Will he be able to come around to pick them up or would it be better if he waited in the car? Talk about all the options.

- *What communication is acceptable?* How often will you speak, text, or email? What would feel comfortable and provide the chance for better interaction—without deluging your husband with anxious messages?

- *What if there is an emergency?* Perhaps one of your children is ill or your mother has an accident. Discuss what happens under these circumstances and what constitutes an emergency.

- *What should we tell the children?* On one hand, they have a right to know what is going on. On the other hand, you don't want them drawn into adult matters. My advice is to be guided by their questions, to aim for honesty, but to tell them as little as possible—especially if you still hope to save your marriage. Remember, you are the experts on your children, what they know already and how best to help them through this difficult period.

- *The other woman?* As you've probably realized, you cannot stop him contacting her. After all, if you are "separated," you will have even less say about his behavior. However, you can still be assertive and ask for what you want. For example: he should not introduce her to the children until he has discussed it with you. Of course, he can say no and you can negotiate.

Coping with a temporary separation

If you've been following the other ideas in this chapter—especially radical acceptance—you will probably feel a sense of relief that you're not thinking about your marriage every second of the day. However, there are still some issues to consider.

- *Focus on eliminating misunderstandings.* When communicating at a distance, without the benefit of body language, a smile, or tone of voice to soften a message, most couples end up misunderstanding each other. So try to keep emails and texts on a business-like basis: "What time should I pick up the kids?" or "How many packed lunches will be needed?" Keep emotionally charged matters for a face-to-face conversation or, at the very least, on the phone. If you get an upsetting text or email from your husband, don't reply straightaway. It might be that you have jumped to the wrong conclusion. Even if he has indeed lobbed a hand grenade, it's not helpful to send one back. Remember the importance of acknowledging, even in emails and texts ("I know you're angry, but ..."), and then reply in as neutral a way as possible. For example: "Could we discuss this when we meet on Wednesday?" If you must communicate something important by email, write a draft and leave it for at least twenty-four hours before sending it. The next day, it might not seem so important or you might decide to tone down the language.

- *Make certain that you are truly giving him space.* I have worked with some women who besieged their husbands, and his family, with texts, emails, and calls during a temporary separation. In some cases, it took a lot of work to get them down to just one email a day. I know you are going to be worrying that out of sight is out of mind. I know you want to know whether he's going to the parent teacher meeting and that issues such as what to do about your cousin's wedding next month seem incredibly pressing. However, be honest with yourself: are you are using this minimal contact to keep a lid on your panic? Unfortunately, you could be putting yourself in the worst of all worlds: a temporary separation that does not feel like one.

- *Be as real as possible.* How do you behave when you do meet up? Should you concentrate on enjoying yourself (although that can seem like sweeping problems under the carpet) or should you have serious conversations (except it can seem like you never have any fun)? Rather than opting for light or heavy, I would like you to be "real." By all means, go out for a drink and enjoy yourself, but if something comes up, talk about it. If you feel like you're walking on eggshells, ask him why or acknowledge what's happening: "You seem upset that I want to go home now." If it's you who's upset, tell him why: "I wonder if you're coming just to tick the box, rather than letting go and enjoying yourself." Even if it creates a moment of unpleasantness, that's better than the alternative, which many couples use: firing off an angry text afterward. Not only is it too late to change plans, for example, having a coffee together before heading to separate homes, but you've wasted an opportunity to communicate better. By being real, you can enjoy yourself, still work on the relationship when necessary but, most importantly, make the most of your time together.

When he comes back

I thought long and hard before deciding on "when" rather than "if" in the heading for this section. Assuming that you have understood why your marriage became vulnerable, improved communication, and been compassionate to both yourself and your husband, I believe he will ask for another chance. Although it is tempting to give a big sigh of relief and let your guard down, think carefully before letting him return home.

Check that he's truly ready

Being away from you and particularly the kids is going to be really hard. He will miss you. If he's living with the other woman, they will have disagreements and fall out and he'll wonder if "his true love" is all he imagined. However, there is a big difference between him taking stock of his life, realizing he's made a mistake, and deciding to put it right, and a knee-jerk reaction. If your life has descended into soap opera, with your husband making big decisions late at night and after a couple of drinks, I would be wary of another spur-of-the-moment choice—even if, in your opinion, it's the right one! Suggest he sleeps on his decision, suggest that you meet up tomorrow and talk it through, suggest that he stays somewhere else for a while—to make certain he's 100 percent sure. In this way, you will not have to listen to your husband's phone pinging with text alerts and see him sloping off to the bottom of the yard to speak to her.

Give him a chance to court you

You have been through one of the biggest challenges that a woman can face. Although you've tried to keep everything together for the children's sakes, you are completely devastated and your self-esteem has taken a real knock. Although taking him back will make you feel momentarily better, your recovery will be more straightforward if you feel he *really* wants you—not just his kids, his home, and a healthy bank balance. Of course, he can promise the moon and the stars, but I expect his words are going to seem rather devalued by now. What counts are actions. So, by all means, give him the green light and tell him you're up for trying again, but he has to win you back by court-ing you, taking you to nice places, and demonstrating that you're a priority.

Discuss the ground rules

Let him suggest what contact he will have with the other woman after he returns home. Ask him if he's sure that he can deliver on that promise. If you're unhappy with his suggestions, keep talk-ing, rather than closing down negotiations altogether. It could be that he's not truly ready or needs a halfway house between her place and coming home, such as staying with his parents, friends, or even renting an apartment. Remember there is no ticking clock and he will value you more if he feels that he has won you over—rather than taken your love for granted.

You might not still want him

It could be that all the work that you've done on yourself has allowed you to step back and look at your relationship through fresh eyes. Time alone might have shown that you can manage on your own. You might even discover that you don't actually want him back.

"After two years of hell, during which I discovered my husband had not one, but two, affairs with coworkers, I can now manage to keep most things in perspective. I no longer react to my feelings the minute I feel them; I try to think about the alternatives instead of assuming the worst; and all of this has led me to have a fantastic relationship with my two sons, and an honest, adult relationship with my parents.

I accept my contribution to what happened, but I no longer feel worthless, not good enough, or to blame in any way for my ex-husband's problems—or for what happened. I understand now that I was a woman who never had any self-esteem, who was codependant and attracted to narcissistic men.

I feel as though I have literally been broken down and rebuilt. It is a very long process, but I feel I am now a balanced 'rounded' person who has her own personality—who makes HERSELF happy as well as everyone else. I discovered that there are things I don't want to change about me—I do care about people, I do like looking after others, but I have to let them grow and be their own people too, and make their own mistakes. I can't smother them to make them love me ...

I'm now in a new relationship with a man I have known all of my life. We met up again about a year ago while I was in therapy, and he knows all about my past. I have never known a man like him, nor had a relationship so equal, so honest, or so respectful— and I really do see him as someone I could spend the rest of my life with."

Final thoughts

Time and time again, I get letters from wives who think, not unreasonably, how can my husband and I bond again if there's another woman in the picture? Therefore, rather than fixing the original problems, the wife puts all her energy into trying to push the other woman out of the way. Guess what? It puts her center-stage and gives her more power than she really has and, if a husband is getting daily reminders about the other woman from his wife, how can he ever forget her?

To make things worse, many wives use tears, anger, recriminations, and shame to try to force their husbands to act. Guess what? This just builds a bigger wall between the two of them. The husband thinks, "We've been working on the marriage and getting nowhere, so I must leave," and the wife complains, "But we haven't even started, because she's in the way." I hope that this book will help you to avoid this trap and show that it is possible to come out of this crisis with your sanity intact and a better understanding of your husband, your marriage and, most importantly of all, yourself.

If you find yourself losing hope and needing more reassurance, I have one closing thought for you. It's human nature to want to concentrate on the nice parts of rebuilding your relationship, such as more cuddles, nights out, and being kinder to each other. However, it is equally important to look at the nasty stuff, for example acknowledging anger and unexpressed hurt or working

on changing communication. In this way, you will be disman-
tling the wall between you one brick at a time (with each positive
interaction), rather than trying to pretend it doesn't exist or looking for magical ways to blast it away.

In effect, you will be able to stare into the darkness, but still
stand firm. Slowly but surely, you will discover some gray among
the black and even a few spots of light. If you can live in the
moment, rather than worrying about next week, month, or year,
you will be able to talk calmly and your husband will respond
better. Slowly but surely, you are developing resilience and that's
a great skill to possess—whatever happens next.

Love Coach's Three Key Things to Remember

- The true test of whether to give up or fight on is whether
  you can still give, even if you're not getting anything
  back.

- Accepting the situation does not mean that you approve
  or that you're giving up, just that you are being realistic
  about your options.

- Sometimes it is best to make a tactical withdrawal, rather
  than risk damaging your love for your husband.

Love Coach's Fifteen Key Things to Remember from Part Two

To help you when you are feeling down or panicking about the other woman, I've gathered together the most important lessons from Part Two to keep you focused, to channel your energy into the most productive activitie, and ultimately to win your husband back.

- Keep calm and don't make decisions that will help you feel better today but set up more problems for tomorrow.

- Aim to be polite and solicitous about your husband's welfare, but don't try to solve his problems for him.

- Once the immediate shock of discovering infidelity has passed, if your life is resembling a soap opera that's probably a sign that you need a fresh approach to resolving this crisis.

- Your husband's behavior will be unpredictable. He's under immense pressure and he does not have the tools to understand or process his feelings and therefore to make sensible decisions.

- Shaming your husband might make you feel temporarily better, but you risk pushing him so far down that, in an effort to feel better, he will indulge in more unhelpful behavior.

- You can't control your husband, but you can ask for what you need, listen to him, and negotiate.

- The other woman must be in a dark place if she thinks another woman's husband is going to turn her life around.

- You cannot control the other woman, but you can control your reaction to her.

- If your husband is really trying to choose between you and the other woman, be the better person and someone with whom he'd want to spend the rest of his life.

- Men find it difficult to communicate in highly charged situations when they feel threatened or vulnerable.

- Accept your feelings, because they are a natural response to a difficult situation, but challenge your thoughts because they could exaggerate the threat and turn a set back into a catastrophe.

- You can't match the excitement of a new relationship, but you can duplicate some of the behaviors and begin to rebuild your loving connection with your husband.

- The true test of whether to give up or fight on is whether you can still give, even if you're not getting anything back.

- Accepting the situation does not mean that you approve or that you're giving up, just that you are being realistic about your options.

- Sometimes it is best to make a tactical withdrawal, rather than risk damaging your love for your husband.

My husband is texting another man

"I was told 'I love you but I'm not in love with you' about a month ago. My husband of seven years simply said that there's very little left in his heart, that he feels very deeply toward me, but this feeling is not 'in love.' He said over and over again that it is not my fault; that I am the most amazing thing that ever happened to him; there's no better wife in the world and I deserve to be happy.

Needless to say, I asked if there's another woman, but he gave me his word there's no woman, that he would never cheat on me with another woman. I should have known then where it was heading. All I could hear was: 'No, I would never cheat on you; it's a different reason altogether; we can still make it work.' How silly I was.

Instead of hearing what he really had to say, but could not, I heard only what I wanted to hear and jumped on the 'Let's fix it' wagon. I got your 'I Love You But I'm Not in Love With You' book, read it twice, acted on it. I pulled out all my not-to-scratch behaviors, dissected them, acknowledged them, unidentified myself with them. But anything and everything I've done was of no use.

I asked again and again about the possibility of another woman, but a firm 'No' was the answer, until I jokingly asked, 'So what, you had an affair with a man?' The silence that followed from his side made my heart stop with fear. Well, he did.

At this particular point, he does not know who he really is. He does not know if he is gay or not (to me, he's afraid to accept it). He talks about trying to bury his memory of enjoyment of the affair and I cannot imagine a worse thing he could do to himself. I've told him 'Your sexuality is not something you can choose; you'll have to find out and accept who you are or you'll bond yourself to a life of unhappiness,' however he replies, 'I can

*choose to bury it and forget about it.' I'm torn in two directions.
I want him to do just that because I love him and desire him, but
I also love him and want the best for him too.*

*From the beginning of our relationship until this second, my
heart grows with love for him day after day: it is so very deep, it is
in every single cell of my body. I was surprised to find out through
this ordeal that, apart from my love being overwhelmingly,
painfully saturating, it is also unconditional, as not for one
millisecond did I feel it reducing, but on the contrary, becoming
stronger after his confession.*

*I accept him as he is and this acceptance makes it horribly
hard for me, as deep inside I know there won't be an 'us' anymore. I'm intentionally trying to prepare myself for the worst outcome, but at the same time it will be the best outcome for him if
he is gay.*

*Everything is all good and clear when rationalization steps in,
but when I have no more power to explain it to myself logically,
all hell breaks loose: feelings of guilt, helplessness, desire to be
with him no matter what, despair, fear of being on my own, fear
of never being able to feel him next to me again, not to feel his
smell, touch, look into his eyes. I can't let go of him, but anything
I'd attempt to do to make him stay would be acting against
nature.*

*He asks for time. I'm planning a three-month journey out of
the country to give him time and space, and also to see how I
can survive on my own. We both are immigrants and have no
other family here apart from each other. Returning back to my
country of birth is not an option; the place where I am now is
my home.*

*How do I stop hoping for the best? How do I stop fooling
myself? How do I put my broken heart back together? How can I
help him? How can I help myself? How do I stop loving him so
much?? How can I get strong, powerful, and invincible again?"*

My answer: It is not often that I receive such a generous letter,
especially from someone whose heart is breaking. All I can
say is that you feel things deeply and, in some ways, that is
a great asset because it can bring a lot of joy, but it doesn't

make for an easy life, because the ability to feel pain is equally strong. So I suppose I wouldn't want you to be strong, powerful, and invincible—because I think that would be denying your feelings and who you truly are. In my opinion, "invincible" means "unfeeling" and "strong and powerful" can easily lack compassion.

So let's look at your options. Sexuality is more complex than just gay or straight—there are a lot of staging posts in the middle. One of the reasons your husband is having trouble labeling himself is because we still live in a world where many people see being gay as shameful. (You mention being immigrants; it could be that distance from his family has given your husband room to explore his sexuality away from their judging eyes.) However, it is equally possible that he is part of a complex tapestry. Believe it or not, there are many heterosexual men who have sex with men. They love women, but get their rocks off with men because they are readily available and offer no-strings sex. There are also men who are bicurious, occasionally dabbling but do not identify as truly gay; bisexual, equally likely to love either sex; and gays who have sex with women—they love men and identify as gay, but have occasional sex with women or even fall in love with a woman. Sorry if I'm confusing you, but sexuality is not a black-and-white thing.

Have a look into an organization called the Straight Spouse Network. They report that about a third of marriages split up on discovery. A third try to stay together, but fail. Another third stay together (but the gay or lesbian partner is allowed outside liaisons). I suppose what I'm saying is that there is no ticking clock. Your husband does not have to self-identify and you don't have to decide on the future of your marriage tomorrow. Keep talking, keep your options open, and talk some more.

Slowly but surely, a way forward will emerge. It could be still as partners, as part of a blended family (where each of you have new partners, but meet up and spend time together), or you could go your separate ways. However, you are in shock at the moment and that's not a good time to decide anything, but the longer you talk, the easier it is to come to terms with the final outcome. So be patient with yourself and your husband.

My husband says he's not gay

Infidelity is hard, but discovering your husband has been unfaithful with another man has another level of shame which isolates both you and him.

"I have been married for 15 years and have two children. Seven years ago I found out that my husband was having affairs with men. We tried counseling, but the counselor did not know how to help us. My husband says he is not gay, but I think he is. I've thought about this every day of my life for the past seven years. I am finally ready to separate from him, but am very scared for my kids. He is a wonderful father and we have a good life, except for the marriage part; we are best friends. I have a few friends who know about our history and they say that I am crazy for staying married to him. I am only married to him for the kids. We have not had sex in years and do not sleep in the same room."

My answer: Your husband has affairs with men, but isn't gay? Does he just help out when they're busy and need an extra pair of hands? OK, enough of the old jokes. I'm sorry to laugh, but the only alternative is to cry and I bet you've done enough of that already.

I would like to think that we live in a sufficiently tolerant society where young men who think they are gay are allowed to experiment and find if that's their true path. Unfortunately, our culture is still full of poison—debates about gay marriage are full of hatred and some churches promise eternal damnation. No wonder lots of potentially gay men find a nice girl, have a family, and pretend to live happily ever after.

But this is what makes me want to scream: what about their poor wives? I don't think anybody else can really understand what you must have gone thorough for the past seven years. And it probably has been pulling you down for even longer: wondering what's wrong with me, why doesn't he want to touch me?

I wish that we could have been having this conversation seven years ago. I would have explained that your husband is so full of self-loathing—from all those negative images from the pulpit and the press—that he can't love himself, let alone another man.

Gay is as much a lifestyle, with loving another man at the center, as a sexuality. Your husband would be categorized as a man who has sex with other men (and, in his case, not his wife). Effectively, at the point you first discovered his activities, you had two choices. You could have decided to separate or that you loved each other enough to put your children's happiness before you own—but that he would have occasional discreet liaisons on the side, within agreed limits, and perhaps you would have taken a lover too. Unfortunately, these issues were fudged at the time and we're seven years down the line. My suspicion is that the second option is no longer viable and why should it be? You need love, affection, and to feel special. I doubt your husband can do that or perhaps he's trying, but you are full of bitterness yourself.

So please feel free to shout: it's not fair. Life has dealt you a horrible set of cards. However, if you hold this pain too close, it will destroy you and your family. So my advice would be to start to mourn for the marriage you wanted, thought you had, and the nice guy you married. You could also look at the websites on the internet designed to help women like you—rather than talking to friends, because how can they understand? Finally, try some counseling to help you move forward.

It might seem bleak, but you have made a difficult decision and this is the start of your recovery. Don't rush into leaving, I would hope that you and your husband can learn to cooperate as coparents, by handling it carefully over a few months, with lots of talking.

Finally, I would like you to be kind to yourself. My guess is that you're beating up yourself for making such a bad choice of husband, but I think you probably made a great choice for a father for your children. After all, he has loved them enough to bury his sexuality (at least partially) and kept the show on the road for seven long years. However, it's time for some honesty with yourselves and each other.

My husband is watching gay porn

From the midnineties, therapists began to see more and more men who were having problems with pornography. There is

217

something about the internet—the novelty of millions of potential fantasy sex "partners" and pornography being constantly available—that tipped many men from using into abusing pornography. Over recent years, I have noticed three important changes:

- Many men have an incredibly ambivalent attitude: they crave porn, but don't like it.

- The more porn is used, the more many men want it. However, there is a problem of tolerance. Where once a pretty girl gyrating in a bikini or straightforward intercourse would be thrilling, tastes are ramped up to provide more stimulation and get the same dopamine high (the reward chemical in the brain). No wonder there has been an increase in pornography in the amount of angry sex (such as men ejaculating over women's faces or forceful intercourse), sadomasochism, and fetishist material.

- Pornography can alter men's sexual tastes.

So what does it mean if your husband has been using gay or ladyboy pornography? It is important to realize that there is not a direct link between fantasy and what we want to do and be. I've come across heterosexual women who watch gay porn, so they can relax and enjoy the male form without having to compare themselves to female porn stars, and gay men who enjoy heterosexual pornography. I discuss why we fantasize and what fantasies reveal about us in my book *Have the Sex You Want: A couple's guide to getting back the spark*.

It is easy to be angry and critical about your husband's viewing. However, the more that you shame him about his porn habits and tastes, the more he will shut down, minimize the problem, or go on the offensive—and try to shame you for spying on him.

I don't think many women understand the central place that masturbation plays in many men's lives. It is a source of pleasure and comfort, a way of unwinding, and going off to sleep, and provides distraction from stress and worry. Unfortunately, if your husband does not talk about his feelings or represses them, they don't just disappear, but pop up somewhere else—like his sexual fantasies. Therefore, it is easy for nonsexual issues and sexual matters to get completely intertwined. So please don't jump to simplistic conclusions, but instead read around the topic and get better informed (see "Further reading").

If you try not to judge but to let your husband talk, you will get a better sense of how much of the problem is his and how much it is a relationship problem and how best to proceed.

Summing up

It is easy to think that the traditional family—mother, father, children under the same roof in a monogamous marriage—is the only way and to overlook the alternatives. The thought of being married to a man who has sex with other men or is bisexual or primarily gay is most probably abhorrent and, indeed, you might be better off ending your marriage and finding someone who wants you—and only you. However, it is important to fully explore your feelings and make certain that this is not just a knee-jerk reaction. Conversely, deciding immediately that "we can beat this," believing your husband's declarations that he can change, and pushing everything underground can often bring more pain farther down the line.

It takes time to recover from the shock of discovery, to mourn the marriage that you thought you had, and to come to terms with this new version of your husband. Most importantly, I would also ask you to consider your needs and wants (for love and sex) and not just those of your children (to have their father living under the same roof). Ultimately, there is no right or wrong solution, but whatever happens you and your husband have a lot of talking to do. The skills I outline in this book—assertiveness, coping with anxiety, and living in the moment—will provide focus and avoid this crisis tipping over into a catastrophe.

Love Coach's Three Key Things to Remember

- Don't rush into making any long-term decisions.
- Try not to take the discovery too personally. It is more about your husband's sexuality than about your desirability.
- Shaming your husband will only add to the shame he already feels and make it harder for the two of you to discuss your options.

By the author

Help Your Partner Say 'Yes': Seven steps to achieving better cooperation and communication, Bloomsbury, London, 2011
How carrots work better than sticks when trying to persuade your partner, and how to come back from crisis point.

How Can I Ever Trust You Again?: Infidelity: From discovery to recovery in seven steps, Bloomsbury, London, 2011
Explains why affairs happen, how to stop your imagination going into overdrive, and why some couples get blocked in the recovery process.

I Love You But I'm Not in Love with You: Seven steps to saving your relationship, Health Communications Inc., 2007
Explains why love changes and how to get back the loving feelings. Essential reading alongside this book.

I Love You But You Always Put Me Last: How to child-proof your marriage, Health Communications Inc., 2014
How men can feel sidelined after children or, worse still, abandoned. Meanwhile, how you can feel resentful about being landed with the majority of the childcare and chores, as well as the impact on your relationship.

Learn to Love Yourself Enough: Seven steps to improving your self-esteem and your relationships, Marshall Method Publishing, 2014
Everything you need to know to start working on yourself and repair your battered self-confidence.

Have the Sex You Want: A couple's guide to getting back the spark, Marshall Method Publishing, 2014
How to reestablish the sexual spark with your husband and let the love flow between you; particularly helpful for couples with two children under five.

By other authors

Full Catastrophe Living: Using the Wisdom of Your Body and Mind to Face Stress, Pain, and Illness, Jon Kabat-Zinn, rev. ed., Bantam Books, New York, 2013
Although principally about physical pain, it does cover emotional distress and its effect on sleep and eating. There is also advice on keeping calm.

The Men on My Couch: True stories of sex, love, and psychotherapy, Dr. Brandy Engler with David Rensin, Berkley Books, New York, 2013
How men and women can easily misunderstand each other when it comes to sex and an explanation of compulsive womanizing, extreme pornography, and male anger.

The New Male Sexuality: The truth about men, sex, and pleasure, Bernie Zilbergeld Ph.D., rev. ed., Bantam Books, New York, 1992
A down-to-earth look at men's relationship with their penises and a book I often recommend to both female and male clients.

The Road Less Travelled: A new psychology of love, traditional values and spiritual growth, M. Scott Peck, Arrow Books, 1990
A self-help classic which explains how avoiding pain only brings greater problems and explores the link between psychology and spirituality.

Sex and the Psyche: The truth about our most secret fantasies, Brett Kahr, rev. ed., Penguin Books, London, 2008
What sexual fantasies tell us about ourselves and the results of the largest-ever survey into our unspoken desires.

Wherever You Go, There You Are: Mindfulness meditation for everyday life, Jon Kabat-Zinn, Hachette Books, 2009
How to be in touch with your real feelings, rather than ignore them and risk being overwhelmed.